WHAT PEOPLE AF

NEW LIFI

These inspiring and touching real-life stories demonstrate how mindfulness and therapy can help to deal with the issues underlying addiction.
Johan Hansen, Founder and President of the New Life Foundation

These inspiring stories demonstrate the transformative power of mindfulness and meditation practice: the power to heal the heart-mind in recovery and beyond. These are real people, real stories, and they give real hope. I recommend this book.
Vince Cullen, Founder of Hungry Ghost Retreats, part-time Buddhist Chaplain at HM Prison Coldingley and visiting Buddhist Chaplain at HM Prison Send

New Life Stories

Journeys of Recovery
in a Mindful Community

New Life Stories

Journeys of Recovery
in a Mindful Community

Hilary H. Carter

AYNI
BOOKS

Winchester, UK
Washington, USA

First published by Ayni Books, 2014
Ayni Books is an imprint of John Hunt Publishing Ltd., Laurel House, Station Approach,
Alresford, Hants, SO24 9JH, UK
office1@jhpbooks.net
www.johnhuntpublishing.com
www.ayni-books.com

For distributor details and how to order please visit the 'Ordering' section on our website.

ISBN: 978 1 78279 663 3

A CIP catalogue record for this book is available from the British Library.

Design: Lee Nash

Printed in the USA by Edwards Brothers Malloy

We operate a distinctive and ethical publishing philosophy in all
areas of our business, from our global network of authors to
production and worldwide distribution.

CONTENTS

Introduction	1
About New Life	3
Mission of New Life Foundation	5
The Stories:	6
Dirty's Story	6
Jamie's Story	15
Gretel's Story	33
Liam's Story	44
Alain's Story	57
Kate's Story	67
Amber's Story	73
Sarah's Story	88
Graham's Story	97
Hugo's Story	107
Hugo's Diary	112
Mindfulness:	143
What Is Mindfulness?	143
Why Meditate?	145
A Short Course in Mindfulness	146
Benefits of Practice	150
Body Scan	151
Top Tips from Meditators	154
Glossary	157
Resources	170
Further Reading	173

This book is dedicated to everybody at the New Life Foundation,
Chiang Rai, Thailand.
www.newlifethaifoundation.com

Do not take lightly small misdeeds,
believing they can do no harm.
Even a tiny spark of fire
can set alight a mountain of hay.
Do not take lightly small good deeds,
believing they can hardly help.
For drops of water, one by one,
in time can fill a giant pot.
– Patrul Rinpoche

Introduction

The mellow sound of the temple bell drifted through the early morning mist. It was 6:30am and I could hear the sound of chanting from the temple in the village. The monks in the local Buddhist temple started their day early, but not as early as the residents of the mindfulness community where I was spending time. Already the community's cows were being milked and people were gathered in the meditation hall for the 6am yoga class.

The breakfast was being prepared, to be eaten in silence in the dining room at 7am. There would just be the sound of crockery and cutlery, the scraping of chairs along the floor and padding of bare feet across the tiled floor. Footwear was always left outside the door in typical Thai tradition.

At 8am all the members of the community meet in the meditation hall, slowly gathering and sitting silently in a circle waiting for the gong to sound so that the 11 hours of noble silence could end. Attending this meeting was compulsory, as was the daily community work. It was referred to as 'working meditation'.

I arrived at the New Life Foundation in Thailand during the last week of November. The registration procedure was rather like what I imagine it must be like to be admitted to prison. I was handed a towel, one set of work clothes, a toilet roll, a set of bed sheets and the key to room number 9. The rooms were located in rows of single-storey terraced bungalows with direct access to the outdoors. The gap under my door was large enough to allow any species of creepy crawly from the jungle to gain access. The floor was concrete and the bathroom was untiled and very basic. Like it or not, this was to be my home for the next 33 days.

At that point I was under the impression that I had come to New Life as a volunteer yoga teacher. It didn't take long to find out that was not the real reason that I was there. I'm a writer. I write about numbers (especially 11:11) and how they can be used as guidance to release the hold of the ego. It was numbers that had led me to New Life in the first place, a mindfulness retreat center situated in the northern province of Chiang Rai. The New Life Foundation is a place where people can come if they are struggling with depression, anxiety, alcoholism, drug addiction, bereavement or more. It's also open to guests and volunteers. In fact, without the volunteers New Life could not operate in the way that it does.

On a Wednesday evening someone from within the community is invited to share their life story. Hearing these stories really affected me. I sat in awe as these brave souls recounted their experiences. That's when I realized that the real reason for me being at New Life was to bring these stories to a wider audience. That is why this book has been written. Ten members of the community have been kind enough to share their stories with me and they form the basis for this book. The stories are true stories. Only a few personal details have been changed to protect identities. Without their willingness to share, this book would not have been written so I would like to take this opportunity to thank them all for their valuable contribution. I would also like to thank all those who helped in other ways to manifest this book.

New Life is a non-profit organization. They do not make any financial gain from the suffering of others. One hundred per cent of the royalties from this book will be donated to help to support some of those who cannot afford to pay for the help on offer at New Life.

Hilary H. Carter

About New Life

New Life Foundation is a mindful recovery community nestled amid the hills and lakes of northern Thailand. The foundation is a registered non-profit organization that offers an affordable learning space for those who would like to work on self-improvement and personal development, and for people who are suffering because of stress, burnout, depression, abuse, and relationship or addiction issues.

The Foundation was founded by Johan Hansen, a Belgian entrepreneur, in June 2010. Johan first discovered the healing powers of mindfulness practice in Thailand. He found it to be an excellent way to cope with the stresses of doing business. Johan continued to study Buddhism and mindfulness at retreats and workshops around the globe, becoming more and more convinced these practices could help those who are struggling on their path towards freedom and happiness.

Johan decided to share his experience by founding a community to help people in need with an affordable, mindfulness-based recovery program. He bought 63 acres of land in Chiang Rai province, near the Golden Triangle, and donated this magnificent property to establish a community where people from all over the world could take the time to start a new life.

The community provides the best possible environment for healing body and mind with mindfulness practice at the heart of the recovery program. There is meditation, yoga, tai chi, sustainable agriculture, natural building, 12 steps, life coaching, mindfulness practice, art therapy, Enneagram, relapse prevention, compassionate sharing, retreats, workshops, and much more. Within the New Life community, everyone is actively engaged in learning from each other: staff, residents and volunteers. Additionally, they believe that while all of us have

3

suffering and problems in our lives, these experiences can be used to gain understanding of ourselves and life in general.

Over the past decades researchers and mental health professionals have been discovering that mindfulness practice can alleviate many kinds of psychological suffering. Mindfulness helps us understand what lies at the root of our behavior and thus it has the power to transform negative habits. We all experience disappointments and difficulties in life but instead of escaping or fantasizing about some other life it is possible to learn to enjoy the life we are living. By becoming more aware of our body, thoughts and emotions we receive signals about what's out of balance. Mindfulness teaches us to respect these signals and welcome them instead of pushing them away.

Mission of New Life Foundation

- To create a recovery community for people who are looking for personal development or who are suffering because of stress, burnout, relationship problems, abuse, depression or addiction.
- To develop a unique mindfulness-based recovery program and offer it at an affordable price.
- To create individualized coaching programs that help our residents discover their potential and develop a healthy and sustainable lifestyle.
- To create an organization where atmosphere, environment and activities all help to cultivate mindfulness and inner growth.
- To create an organization where the staff members have a love for learning and spiritual growth and are role models in living a mindful life.
- To create a sustainable farm that will offer healthy food choices to all of our members, provide an opportunity to our members to practice mindfulness in physical work and provide an additional income for the foundation.
- To become an educational center for everyone who wishes to learn about mindfulness or other activities which cultivate inner growth. New Life will also allow other organizations to use the facilities to organize workshops and seminars on mindfulness-related subjects.

The Stories

Dirty's Story

I've got quite a lot of tattoos on my body. Some of them I regret, like the ones of a syringe and a guy hanging himself, but others I'm really glad I've had done like the train wreck and a portrait of my mom from when she was young. I really love my 11:11 tattoos. I've got that on my back as well. On my back it's written as 'eleven-eleven' but on my wrist it's done as '11:11' just like it appears on the clock. I've had it done twice because that has been such an important number in my life. I've also got my family crest on my arm. My family has German roots and when we reach the age of 18 each member of the family is given a 24-carat gold ring with the family crest on it. When I reached 18 my dad said, "I'm not giving you the ring because you'll just sell it and use the money to go and buy drugs." He was right. That's what I would have done because I've had addiction issues all my life.

Eventually I did get given a ring when I was 21 and, just as my dad predicted, I used it to pawn it for drugs. But then once when it was pawned I forgot that the interest was due and by the time I got back to the pawn shop it had gone, been melted down. So in memory of the ring I got a family crest tattoo and marked it 24k.

My life has not been easy. All my life I have struggled with self. It has manifested in addictions and other attachments to stimulation, sedation, anything just to keep me distracted, to change the way that I feel. Mostly I've done drugs and alcohol to keep a lid on things. I started early, at the age of 13. In those early days I inhaled gasoline, butane, whiteout, whatever, anything for a cheap escape. I remember vividly the time I had my first drink and it was like magic. It numbed me and I couldn't wait to do it again. I wanted to do it as often as possible.

As I grew up I felt insecure, inadequate, I felt I had nobody I could talk to. My mom was around but I couldn't really communicate with her. It's not that I couldn't trust her but… well, actually I didn't trust her. She used to leave me with babysitters when she went out to work and things happened with them, things that shouldn't have happened.

I remember them trying to get me to see counselors when I was really young, like 8 years old, but I wouldn't go. I didn't want to talk to strangers about my feelings. I was already going to group meetings for the children of alcoholics by that age, but I had no interest at all in being at the group because my mom's alcoholism didn't seem to affect me at all. I mean she was there most of the time. I remember her being drunk and silly sometimes. I can remember one alcohol-fueled incident when we were at my grandparents' house in Phoenix and my mom got really drunk and she was getting mouthy and my grandma asked her to leave. She was giving everyone the finger as she left. I knew it was the alcohol and people didn't like drunk people being around.

Drugs and alcohol became a big part of my life from the gate. I had probably only got drunk six or seven times before they sent me to a rehab. Looking back I can see I was an addict even before I started. It came to a head when I was at a Grateful Dead show at the Meadowlands. I consumed an insane amount of alcohol and drugs. There was no hiding it from my parents. While on 'probation' a friend had given me half a bottle of whiskey called Yukon Jack. It's a bit like Southern Comfort but higher proof. I was pissed they were trying to control me. I drank it all. I was blackout drunk. I do remember throwing the bottle down and it broke. I rubbed my face and arms with the glass and cut myself pretty badly. It was really a cry for attention because deep down I didn't really want to die. I was behind the train station when I did it, then stumbled to the phone and must have called 911. Something pushed me because I was bleeding pretty bad. I don't really remember who I called. Maybe the police, maybe the hospital, maybe family? It was all a haze but whatever, I ended up in the hospital.

This happened at about the time that my dad had just moved back in with us. They first split up when I was 4 and finalized the divorce when I was 5. Dad was an alcoholic too. The doctor told him that if he kept on drinking he would die from liver damage. He was really bloated and looked terrible. He managed to get sober though and then he convinced my mom to get treatment a few years later. I had lived with him for a year in Miami. So my mom got sober too but she continued to suffer from depression and so she searched for other things to help her to feel better.

She was reading Dianetics, the Ron Hubbard books, some Scientology crap and she tried meditation too but nothing seemed to work for her. She was always crying, always in tears. Alcohol was her solution to dealing with life and when that was taken away she felt empty. She just couldn't see any joy in life.

My first treatment center was a lot of fun. It was like summer camp. I learned how to play table tennis really well. But what I really liked was the meditation. We had daily guided meditations and I remember following them and really feeling good. The guy was saying "Follow the orb of light as it rises up above the blue sea and hear the waves lapping onto the shore" and all that felt like good stuff. It felt great. I got high the day I left there. I thought it was by choice, because I wanted to. I wouldn't feel that deep peace through meditation again until I stopped drugs and alcohol sometime later.

I got expelled from public school for cutting class and fighting. They sent me to a special school for emotionally disturbed children. There were only about a hundred of us in the whole school, about ten per class. It was a behavior modification kind of place. We'd be bussed in from all over northern New Jersey. Each morning the bus would come and I used to be the last to get picked up and the first to be dropped off which was good. Some of those kids had really serious problems. One guy there had some baking soda and he pulled out this bag of cocaine and started cooking up some crack in the back of the bus. By the time the bus reached school some of the kids had turned blue. They had overdosed and were rushed to the hospital. I tried crack later that year. I went there not knowing a lot about drugs but 'monkey see, monkey do', I guess. It was quite a lenient place. We were even allowed to smoke at school as long as we had a letter of permission from our parents. My mom figured cigarettes were less harmful than the other things I could (and was) getting into.

My English teacher would read us the required books. We called it 'Bedtime with Bernie'. He had grown up in New York and was quite a character, a great guy. I remember him reading *Catcher in the Rye* to us in his New York accent. It was great. He read to us rather than make us try and read to him because quite a few of the kids had problems reading and would take away from the story.

The principal of the place was ex-marine and we had a decent amount of fighting at school. He said, "If you want to fight, come to me and I have boxing gloves and you can put on the gloves and go for it, three rounds of one minute each." Later on that same day I found a guy willing to fight. We told the principal and met him in the gym later that day. He gave us these really heavy gloves and I remember at the end of the first one-minute round, my arms were so tired that I could hardly raise my arms to hit him. It wasn't fun at all.

I was 16 when my mom died. She had cancer. They cut out half of one of her lungs and when she went back for a check a year later they checked from her shoulders to her waist but if they had just moved millimeters down they would have seen all these other tumors, all in her lower intestines. It was painful for her not being able to breathe but as she only had one and a half lungs she thought she had less lung capacity and that's why she couldn't breathe so well. She used to smoke but she gave up. She was only 46. I know now that she just gave up on life.

I felt guilty after she died because I was supposed to be sober but I was drinking with my friends in secret so I went to the meetings in the self-help groups but they wanted me to believe in a Higher Power and I couldn't. I remember going into the forest and looking up at the skies and saying "If there is a God then prove it to me now, send a strong gust of wind to show me that you are there and you can hear me." I was shouting out to the universe for answers. "Give me a flash of lightning, anything to prove that you're there and you can hear me." Nothing happened. I was raised Lutheran. It's Christian, Martin Luther, the guy who said it's not about heaven and hell, it's about being of service. I knew the stories that they told us weren't true so I wanted to know who God really was. Was God a being? I didn't get my sign, no gust of wind and so I went back to drinking and this time I started regularly using heavy drugs. I spent the years after Mom's death getting high. I was shooting coke and heroin. I took PCP for a year. That stuff took its toll on my brain and body though. That is one hell of a nasty drug.

I moved to Phoenix because I thought it would be good to get away from New Jersey. It took me 10 minutes to find a contact for drugs. Within a month I was back in a treatment center, got kicked out for drinking, went back, finished the program and then lived in a halfway house for 10 months where half the residents were drug addicts and the other half were convicts re-entering society. I learned a lot of things at that place like how to cook and make my bed. I grew up fast. I got a job in a little mom-and-pop paint store but I started smoking pot again which led me back to heroin. I ended up stealing from my paint store, a paint sprayer, high-end brushes, anything I could sell quickly. I felt terrible about that because the family in the store were such nice people. I have since made amends by paying them back every cent I took.

After the halfway house I bought a house with my aunt. My mom had left me some money in her will. My aunt said it would be a good idea to invest it so we bought this cute little house in Phoenix for $20,000. The only problem was it was right in the worst area for a newly sober person to move. The connection I found when I first moved to AZ lived under a bridge a few blocks away. I did well for a little while, got heavily involved in the rave scene, just doing a bit of pot and ecstasy every once and a while, staying away from the hard drugs. Actually I must say those couple of years were some of the best times in my life. I was hanging around with this guy Bam and he was all about fun. We listened to Breakbeat. We were music snobs. We danced and lived like there was no tomorrow. Another tattoo on my chest: "Live Fast, Dream Hard".

Those good times didn't last though. I started doing dope again and when my aunt found out she wrote me a letter telling me that the house would have to be sold. I was given 2 weeks to get out and find somewhere else to live. I can't blame her for selling it. Within a month it had become a crack house. When a friend named Freddy died from an overdose that was it for her. I came to around 6:30am, then I found him lying there dead and I called 911. I then called his sister to let her know. That was really hard but I just did it. I had to tell her that his body would be at the city morgue so I called and said, "Is this Freddy's sister?" and she said "Yes". When I told her what had happened she gasped and dropped the phone. Her husband picked up the phone and I gave him the details. Freddy did speed and other drugs but he wasn't into heroin. His dealer was out of speed so he had me get cocaine for him. Later my dealer had run out of cocaine so he said "Get me some heroin." We were already fucked up and high. He had 20mg valium which a friend had given him and that's a really strong dose. And on top of that we were drinking whiskey which together is dangerous but to add heroin on top, no wonder he died. I blamed myself, believing I should have known the heroin would kill him. It was part of the equation but really it was the combination that had killed him. Alcohol, opiates and diazepines together? A totally lethal cocktail. I had a lot of guilt over that for a while. I just feel that I should have told him to be careful: 'Don't do it all together, go slow.' But I was thinking about myself.

His family came to get the few things he had that we didn't pawn. When they left I looked up and saw that it was exactly 11:11. I mean, what made me look up at the clock at that time? That was the first time it kind of smacked me in the face, the 11:11. But that was just the first 11:11 wake-up call, with many more to come.

When I first moved out I slept in the car port and this lady was walking down the street with a dog and she started yelling at me and told me I couldn't sleep here. I said "Bitch, this is my house" and went to get out my ID with the address on it but she didn't believe me and ran off. I decided I'd better get out before the police showed up. There were warrants out for my arrest. So I started sleeping on the streets. I had nowhere to go and a drug habit. I was sleeping in the bushes and this was the hottest summer in AZ on record. I would beg for money, or wash people's car windows. I had a tank top on and I got seriously burned and my skin was all blistered. I couldn't shower so the blisters popped and got infected so my whole body was oozing pus. It was when I got my nickname Dirty.

The people I met out there often died on the street. They stopped breathing, turned blue, white face. If I was there when they went down I gave them mouth to mouth and they would stay alive. Once I spent almost an hour giving this guy mouth to mouth and when he came round he was really angry with me, not knowing what I just did for him. The next day I was panhandling on the corner and he said "Get lost, this is my corner." I said "Dude, I saved your life" and he just punched me in the face and said "Get off my corner." Those were my friends. There was also Little Al, the first guy I got heroin from and his partner Chip. Steve's girlfriend Cathy was a hooker. She had no teeth, just these little black stubs where her teeth used to be. I don't know who picked her up but she would make money. She was a sweetheart though. I remember one day I found a wallet and it had 180 dollars in it and she said "You're going to have to give me some of that or I'm going to have to tell everyone" so I gave her $40 out of it to keep her quiet and she called it hush money.

I'm getting sidetracked here. I really just want to tell you about the 11:11 because I know that you have a real interest in that number. I saw 11:11 many times while I was living on the streets. During my rave days I had a friend called KJ who was a trance DJ from Bangladesh. We didn't really like his music but he was a cool guy. He told us about 11:11. We were high on something at the time and I can't remember everything he said but I remember thinking 'I'm going to begin seeing 11:11 and it shouldn't be ignored when I see it because it's going to mark some sort of change.' I think what he was really saying was about some opening in time/space because that's what a lot of people say 11:11 is about. I tried to read about it online years later but to me it wasn't relevant to what I was experiencing. Others say it has to do with the whole magic thing and parallel universes.

I just felt that seeing it would mark change is coming. Once I got that idea then I started seeing it everywhere. It wasn't like I would be looking for it or waiting for the time to change. I'd just walk into a house and see the clock – 11:11. It was happening here and there and every time I saw it I thought it was cool.

When I hit the streets I became desperate to find a better way to live. I was dying on the streets. I needed to see that gust of wind or lightning bolt. I was seeing 11:11 more and more often. It popped up everywhere all the time. One day I knew it was near my birthday because my birthday is in November. I asked this guy "What's the date today?" and he said "It's 11/11." I was going to call my dad to ask him to send some money for my birthday, that's why I needed to know the date.

Anyway, there was another 11:11. I kept at it and got enough money together for more drugs. As I walked away from the dealer with my heroin I noticed the time flashing on a large digital display clock. It was 11:11 on 11/11!

Later that day me and a friend decided that we would rob a drug dealer. It's pretty serious to steal from a drug dealer and I was afraid of doing it and I thought 'If we do it we'll have to get out of town.' But I was desperate. I figured I could sell some of it to pay my way to California. I was worrying about it and then when I turned the corner there was another clock flashing 11:11 again. I stopped sharp because it was really weird to see it again. Was time staying still at 11:11? It took me a while to figure out the clock was an hour off. It was actually 12:11. Still, it means that I had seen 11:11 twice on 11/11. Later that afternoon some kids asked me to go buy them some beer because they were too young to get served. They said if I bought them the beer I could keep the change. I thought 'Great, that's an easy bag of dope' so they gave me 20 bucks and I bought their 12-pack. With tax it came to $8.89. The change was $11 and 11 cents! Another 11:11 on 11/11! It had my full attention by now.

That evening I panhandled this Christian guy and he just said to me that there's a light in every human soul and that doing drugs and drinking, the light would eventually go out. He said, "When the light goes out there would be nothing to live for, but I can see that you still have a light in you." Then he asked if he could pray with me. I took in what he said about the light thing but I also knew that if I said 'Screw you, I don't want you to pray for me' then he wouldn't give me any money. So I said okay and I let him pray. After the prayer he gave me all the loose change that was in his car. He poured a cup of coins in my hand. I counted it. It was 11 dollars and 11 cents. My mind was blown. Another 11:11 slap in the face. I'd been looking for that gust of wind or a flash of lightning to prove the existence of a Higher Power for many years and nothing had happened. Now all these 11:11s were happening on 11/11.

I knew I needed to stop what I was doing. Not only was I killing myself out there, I was hurting my friends and family and being a total menace to society. I knew many addicts/alcoholics cleaned up through taking the 12 steps, but my problem was always 'What about having to believe in God?' All those synchronicities around the number 11:11 on November 11th was a pivotal day. The message was clear: There is something here. There is something better for me. There is a Higher Power. Make the change, have faith.

At last I could believe in a power beyond myself. I could finally surrender. I got clean. I believe that I was living in my lower self all those years. My self-will without God is full of ego, selfishness and self-pity. I live in fear and am dishonest and frequently get angry with others. Now I can live on a higher plane through God's will. For me God's will is living with compassion, love, kindness and empathy. Not being afraid to be honest. Taking life as it is and being okay with it. Not trying to change it or the way I feel about it.

There's a lot going on in my life at the moment, lots of difficult and challenging stuff. All that I have learned about mindfulness is helping me through it though. I try to remain present. Sitting with fear and anger instead of letting it spin out of control. I'm rolling with the punches with a slight Buddha smile. I still see 11:11 and every time I see it I smile because I know it is a wink from God.

Jamie's Story

I was born and raised in a small town in southern Ireland, the only son in a family of girls, the youngest of five children. My father had always wanted a son so I was very much a wanted child. I was brought up in a house on a housing estate. Like many of these council estates, it was a pretty rough place to live. My father was an odd job man, doing anything he could to bring in money to feed us. He had a ladder and would get on his bike .

with the ladder on his shoulder and go window cleaning. Sometimes he worked as a builder's laborer. Later on he worked as a printer, printing leaflets and T-shirts using a screen printing technique. My mum didn't have a job. Mostly she was a stay-at-home mum, a really good and caring mother who cooked us meals every day, lots of home cooking and care and affection. She cuddled me a lot. But Dad was quite different, the complete opposite in fact. He would discipline us really harshly, beating us with anything that was at hand. I never knew when he would erupt. It could happen any time and it would be over absolutely anything. Sometimes it was over nothing so you just wouldn't know when the outburst was going to come. It could be anything at all, like if he caught me crying or something. He would freak out that I was crying and then he would say, "I'll give you a reason to cry" and then the violence would ensue. When he got into one of his rages he would start punching and lashing out at me and my sisters. He would just lose it completely and it didn't matter that we were small kids, he'd just go crazy and hit us with incredible violence. He was totally out of control when he was in one of his rages and it was really frightening. It's not just the pain of the beating that was hard to take, it was the constant stress of being on red alert. All the time I was worrying about the next blow to the head... always watching my back if you know what I mean.

My father had come from a disadvantaged background himself. He had a really tough upbringing. He never really talked about his father but I just found out quite recently that his dad – my grandfather – had spent most of his life in a psychiatric hospital so he wasn't around for my dad. I understand now that my dad probably found parenting particularly difficult because he had no role model himself. Because his dad wasn't around he lived with his mum and they both used to be begging on the street for food and stuff because they were so poor. This was back in the 1950s. They had a house but they had no income so therefore they had no food. They used to rummage in the big bins at the back of hotels and collect the waste food that had been chucked out. Eventually my dad was taken away from his mum by the authorities and he was put into a home run by the Christian Brothers. His mum didn't want him to go so I guess you could say that he was stolen from her. The Christian Brothers was a Catholic orphanage. You might have heard of it because recently there was a big court case as it had gradually become apparent that many of the children at that particular home had been victims of sexual abuse. I'm pretty sure that my dad was abused but he just won't talk about it. He won't even mention it. Even when it was all over the front pages of the newspapers my dad remained silent and we knew better than to push him for his opinions or an account of his actual experiences. At the age of 12 he left the home and started work. He has worked all his life and he's still working now. I think he has a fear of poverty after those early days spent rummaging in those bins.

My mum's background was much better than my dad's. Her father was a fisherman and they lived by the beach and as far as I know she had a good upbringing. Certainly she experienced nothing like the difficulties that my father had encountered.

I'm sure his background partly accounted for his violent outbursts. I remember once he went for my mum and got her by the throat and so I picked up a chair to throw at him. I couldn't handle him hurting her. She left him numerous times during my childhood because she was trying to protect us, all of us, not just me. He went for my sisters too. I remember my mum would be shouting "Don't hit them on the head!" because he always went for the head and I think she was afraid that he might knock us out, cause brain damage or even kill us. Jesus, he hurt me so often I'm surprised I did survive. Once he took a swing at me with a big metal rake and it got lodged in my leg and I know my mother left him over that particular incident. Each time after he had lashed out and lost it and had beaten me around the place he would, like, come back to me all upset. He would be sobbing like a baby and he'd say he was really sorry and he'd ask me for forgiveness. Then I would start feeling sorry for him.

As a small child I remember wanting to kill my father, not myself. It was later in life that I wanted to end my own life. I was a sensitive and emotional child but I couldn't show it because I was a boy and I had to behave like a boy, not a pansy. I tried to behave in the way that my father expected, always trying to be the son that he wanted.

Life was awful. Every day when I came home from school I had to go and help Dad in the shed and I used to hate that. I used to be shitting myself. I used to be in bits but I had to go or I'd get a beating. The minute I walked through the door after school he'd call me and I had to go out to that shed. I'm telling you, I couldn't wait to leave home and get away so I left as soon as I turned 17. By that age I was already into substance abuse. It really began at the age of about 12 or 13. I started getting drunk. The first time I got drunk was on port. Me and a friend used to doss off school and we met a guy who let us use his mobile home to hide in when we were bunking off. It was such a good feeling to get drunk and I wanted to do it again and again but of course I was only 13 so it wasn't easy getting hold of alcohol. I had no money and I couldn't get served with alcohol in the shop at such a young age. But I started living for those times when I could get hold of some booze and when I had it I would just drink and drink. It went straight down the hatch. Although I was mostly drinking beer and cider at that age, my favorite drink was neat whiskey or vodka. By the age of 16 I was going out clubbing quite regularly and had more access to alcohol and also to ecstasy. That was my favorite drug.

At 17 I moved to Liverpool to train as a screen printer. I returned home after training and there was a job waiting for me but I only lasted a week because I was taking so much drink and drugs that I couldn't hold down the job. The ecstasy was starting to take its toll on me and the cannabis too. I was taking candy pollen which is a really potent form of cannabis. There was a lot of it around at that time. I got it from various dealers and through friends. There was a drug network in the town and I gradually got more and more used to dealing with drugs and hanging out with the druggies. Ecstasy was my drug of choice. The first time I took it was like 'Oh my God, what is this?' It's called ecstasy for a reason. When you take it you feel ecstatic, your eyes start rolling in your head, music sounds amazing, colors are mad and you just feel really high. Those were the days because it was pretty clean back then. You could take it with confidence because you knew what you were going to get. I wouldn't trust it these days.

I was only 20 when I went into my first treatment center. My mum and dad sent me. They found out I was on drugs after I tried to sell my music system and my weights to my dad. They were such precious possessions that they knew I must be desperate for money. Not only that but they had also noticed that money had gone missing in the house. I'm ashamed to say that I had stolen from my own parents. So that's when they realized and they thought 'Oh my God, he's doing drugs.' They didn't realize it until that point and I was 20 years old and had been getting out of my head for almost 7 years. I was in a bad state physically, falling apart, down to 6 and a half stone. I was wasting away in front of their eyes because I wasn't eating. When they got me into the rehab center they could only feed me corners of toast as my stomach had shrunk so much. I was taking so much ecstasy that I couldn't eat because of the comedown. If I took ecstasy on a Friday it would take me until the Monday to come down. The after-effect was awful so I kept taking it to stop me from coming down. That's the downside of the drug. You hit this depression. When I come down I can't bear being in the world, it's like everything is dark and I just want nothing to do with anything. You see, when you're in ecstasy everything is light but the pendulum swings the other way when you come down from the high. That's the price to pay. There's always a price to pay.

Anyway, this treatment center was private. It cost thousands of pounds to stay there. I got a grant towards it and my parents paid some but I still owe a bit to the center. It's a place run for profit, not like New Life. Unfortunately a few weeks after I was admitted my best mate was killed in a car crash. A group of them were going to a party and they were out of their heads and crashed the car. That killed me, losing Greg. In fact I wish it had been me that was killed because the emotional pain was overwhelming. Three of those in the car died and two survived. One of the girls and another guy died. Greg, my best mate, was just about to turn 18. I was cracking up over it but the doctors wouldn't let me out to see him on his deathbed. I'm kind of glad about that now because I heard he was in a really bad way and I didn't really want my last memory of him to be a bad one. They let me out for the funeral but I had already decided that I was going to go to the funeral whether they let me or not and I didn't care if they didn't let me back in. So they let me go and then I returned for treatment, the usual sort of stuff: the 12 steps program, group therapy, meetings and seminars.

I stayed in there for 30 days and there was an aftercare program for a further 2 years so I attended that for a couple of months but then I had a bit of a crisis. I ended up cutting my wrists because I was so depressed. I did it in my bedroom, a long cut up my arm from the wrist with a razor blade. As soon as I had cut my arm open the blood hit the ceiling and I freaked out when I saw how much was coming out. I panicked. There was blood everywhere and it was gushing out. I ran to my parents' bedroom. They got such a shock because I was standing in the doorway covered in blood. I really just wanted everything to end. I realize that I wasn't right in my head. Greg had died and I had stopped taking my prescription drugs. The doctor had prescribed me some stuff but I hadn't taken them so I was on nothing, no antidepressants or anything. Anyway, my dad took one look at me and rushed me to the emergency room at the hospital and in the morning I looked at my arm and it was all stitched up. I didn't remember it being stitched. I think I had lost consciousness. The next morning I convinced them I was fine so I left. I didn't want to be in the psychiatric hospital. They let me out because the bleeding had stopped. It had been a really deep cut. I have had lots of tattoos done to hide the scarring.

Personally I blame the antidepressant that I had been prescribed for that suicide attempt. It's a drug called Seroxat which has been taken off the market now because so many people on it have committed suicide and self-harmed on it. It's crazy because it seemed to exacerbate those tendencies in people that were already that way inclined. I was also put on Xanax which is a bit like valium. I started abusing that straight away because, like, well it felt so nice! I took way over the prescribed dose. I just started lots more drugs after that suicide attempt and I was drinking even more heavily than before and smoking cannabis and taking my prescription tablets and magic mushrooms. I wasn't taking so much ecstasy at that time. Something changed within me around that age – I was 20 – because for the first time I started going into myself and not doing the party scene. I started just using by myself and doing aerosols and that, you know, like glue sniffing, sniffing anything I could get my hands on. I also took mushrooms and acid. I remember once when I was tripping on acid I looked in the mirror and my face was melting. It was crazy. My friend – who had taken a tab from the same batch as me – was rubbing his hands together because he was hallucinating and he thought there was a fire in the middle of the room. That particular trip was a bad one for me. I was just freaked out of my head and I spent most of the time sitting in the corner of the room, just one of those bad trips. I didn't know where I was. It was scary.

I was gradually getting worse and I had taken to locking myself in my room. I locked myself away for days. I even pissed in a plant pot because I wouldn't want to come out for anything, not even to use the bathroom. One day when I was locked in my room and isolating myself I remember looking in the mirror and hating myself so much that I ended up burning myself with a cigarette all over my face and my arms. There were craters all over my face from where I had held the burning cigarette against my skin. I was in a right state. I was destroyed, covered in cigarette burns and deeply depressed. I didn't want to carry on living. Eventually my sister got into my bedroom and found me and I was taken back inside the psychiatric hospital for a couple of months.

They put me on suicide watch and I could only have a cigarette with someone next to me because they were concerned that I would go and burn myself again. After a few months they let me out of the hospital but I still wasn't in a very good way so my parents arranged for me to be taken to another private clinic. One night at this private clinic I developed an abscess on my tooth and it was agony so I went to ask for a paracetamol but the guy on duty rang my mum and said that I was demanding drugs. Ringing my mum at that time in the early hours of the morning just because I needed a paracetamol? What a dickhead.

I can't remember how long I was in that particular place but I do remember how I felt when I was released and returned to my family. I seriously didn't want to be alive. I used to sit in the car and not put my seat belt on because then if it crashed I would be killed. I just wanted to end the pain I guess. If you think about it I had been out of my head, not in reality since the age of 13. I had lived in a drug or alcohol haziness for 7 years. When I came out of the center I wasn't on any drugs. I was in reality without the protection of that haziness and it wasn't a good feeling.

Anyway, I worked on and off during the next few years, doing any work that came my way. Sometimes I worked with my father painting and decorating. He paid me by the day so at the end of each day I had a wad of cash and he would drop me at the pub and I would go and spend the whole lot on drink. In the morning I'd fall into the work van stinking of drink ready for the next day's work and the next wad of cash so that I could get drunk again.

By this time I wasn't living at home anymore. I had found myself a flat but I soon got kicked out for being in a state and not paying rent. All my money went on drink and drugs. Eventually I couldn't get a flat because I had no deposit or references so I ended up homeless. That's when one of my good friends managed to get me into the homeless hostel. By this time I was 27 years old. It was in that hostel that I took heroin for the first time. I met a girl I vaguely knew and she was an addict. I'd never taken it before but at this time in my life I wasn't thinking right. That's probably because I had been on the streets. Physically, mentally and emotionally I was drained. I got kicked out of the hostel for using as it was against the rules. So then I ended up in a wet house where you're allowed to use but I got kicked out of there too after 8 or 9 months because I wasn't paying rent. It was the usual story. Any money I had went on drugs and booze. That took priority over the rent. Also, I got arrested a few times when I was in there because I had drugs inside, and apparently I kept falling down the stairs when I was out of my head. I can't remember that happening. It was around about this time that I cut my wrists again, not to kill myself but just out of desperation. I was demented. I didn't know what I was doing. I got stitched up again so I had even more scarring on my arms. The staff at the hostel took me up to the hospital and while I was in there they packed my bags and they were sitting there by the door when I was discharged. They told me that they were sorry but they just couldn't keep me any longer because they were afraid that I was going to die in there. They kept expecting to find me dead in bed or lying dead at the bottom of the stairs after falling down them.

So then I was homeless again. I had nowhere to go. Sometimes I slept on people's couches or in a squat. Many times I just wandered the streets, sleeping in shop doorways just wrapped in my coat trying to keep warm. I didn't have a sleeping bag or anything and some nights it was so cold. Then the rain and wind would start, but I was so out of it on heroin that I was just existing day to day. The only thing that mattered was getting my next fix. I don't know how I survived. I didn't have the money to feed my habit so I was sick a lot. What happened is that I would score, shoot up and get a high and then when I started coming down the withdrawal symptoms would start, like a mini cold-turkey, caused by giving up drugs and alcohol abruptly rather than gradually. I needed more heroin to stop the withdrawal symptoms which were dreadful. I would be sweating, all my muscles ached, I felt sick and clammy and so on but as I didn't have any money I couldn't score. I tried to scavenge from other addicts but that wasn't always possible. I went through all this sickness while on the streets. It was the pits, being ill and having nowhere to go. As I could only get heroin every few days, during the in-between times I injected vodka, brandy, crushed-up valium and other stuff. I would inject anything. I wasn't afraid to put a needle in. I was addicted to the needle as much as I was to the drugs.

My family was aware of my situation and they took me back in a few times to try and cold turkey me and one of those times I took all the tablets I could find in the house, things like my mum's tranquilizers. I found about 80 of her tablets in the bathroom cabinet. The doctor had put her on them after she had a kind of breakdown. I feel responsible for that. My poor mum, what I've put her through. I'm sure she wouldn't be on them if it wasn't for me. I also found my dad's medication. He was on heavy painkillers for a back injury so these were pretty heavy duty morphine-based tablets. I took all the tablets I found in the house in one go. After that incident my parents always made sure that the bathroom cabinet was kept locked when I was around.

I started having seizures and fits because of the way I had been mistreating my body. I had loads of them but they have scanned my brain and it seems as if I have no lasting damage, thank God. I remember having a seizure in the doctor's waiting room when there were about 20 people in there. The last thing I remember before waking up in hospital is lying on the floor with the doctor holding my head.

I had a girlfriend for a while. She was an addict too. She was trying to stay clean but I wanted to use with her. I didn't want to use on my own. I wanted it to be a shared experience. My girlfriend had taken me back to her place to try and get me together and I had a seizure at her place and ended up back in hospital. Things didn't work out with her. It wasn't a healthy relationship. We split up and I was back on the street yet again.

I was homeless for about a year that time. It was really, really miserable. I had bronchitis, then pneumonia and then I ended up in hospital with pleurisy. That was hell. It was so painful, like a spear going through me. I couldn't move. My lungs are still scarred from that illness. Once I was so desperate for drugs that I tried to rob from a chemist at knife point. I got chased out with a metal bar by the women behind the counter. I was picked up later in the day for that by the police and I was charged with attempted robbery. In their evidence when the case came to court the women said that my face was green and they didn't know what to do because they could see how sick I was, so unwell.

They were right. In fact I don't know how I have survived, how my physical body has managed to stay alive. There was one time when I relapsed and I bought three bags of heroin and shot it all up. For a whole week I was puking up black shit. I was so ill I wasn't able to go out and buy some more.

I'm sure a lot of my problems stem from the sexual abuse that happened when I was a boy. I had approached the subject of abuse in my first treatment center and it was like it wasn't even there. I had completely blacked it out of my memory. It used to happen down in the shed. It was my dad's friend. It went on pretty much every day after school for about a year and a half.

I don't know how I blocked it out. I guess by taking lots of drugs. I never told a soul about what had happened. I just zipped my mouth shut. In the treatment center I wasn't on drugs and this was the first time I had been drug free since the age of 13. Through therapy I realized that I had started getting out of my head shortly after the abuse started and had continued being in a drugged state until I started treatment at the age of 20. When the drug haze started to clear then the memories began to come back again but I didn't want those memories back.

I was only 11 when the abuse started. I would be down in the shed doing screen printing when this man would come in and do things and that's the real reason that I had to give up the printing job because I know it sounds a strange thing to say but the smell of the paint reminded me of those awful times, sort of acted as a trigger. They were such bad memories.

How can a child process something like that happening? How can we? It's just so shocking... we can't process it at that age. All we can do is to just stuff it. I went through years of guilt, believing that it was my fault, that somehow I was to blame for the abuse happening. It was only when my sister had her little boy and as he started getting older and got to around that age when it happened to me that I thought 'Hang on, what if that was happening to him? He couldn't be responsible for that at his age.' I saw my nephew and realized that a child of that age couldn't possibly be held responsible – he was still only a little boy! I had felt all that guilt but it wasn't me who ought to feel guilty but my abuser. All the feelings and mixed emotions were there deep inside me all the time but I kept everything down with drugs and alcohol. The counselors at one of the treatment centers that I attended quite recently were very helpful and they supported me when I decided to find the man responsible, so even though it was years after the event I went and reported it to the authorities. That was pretty awful because the policeman who was interviewing me wanted me to go into details, asking me to tell him exactly what this man had made me do. I wasn't expecting that. That just destroyed me. I had to describe all the details and it was excruciating. After describing what had happened I went to town on myself. I started using more, drinking more, trying to put the lid back on I suppose you could say. However, in the end the police found the guy who did it. They went knocking on his door. He denied it of course, said it wasn't abuse because all he had been doing was teaching me stuff about sex. He never got locked away but it was good that it was finally out in the open.

Not long after the court case and when my family saw the state I was in they arranged to send me to the Thamkrabok monastery in Thailand. It's a place run by Buddhist monks where people can go and detox, go cold turkey and get off drugs. My sister had heard about it on the radio, some program interviewing people who had been there so my sister wrote down the details for me and asked me if I would go. I tell you I was so far down and out that I would have tried anything so obviously I agreed. The next day my family told me that they had bought my plane ticket but I had completely forgotten that I was going. I said "I'm not going to Thailand" because I had forgotten about it. I kept on forgetting everything because my memory was shot to pieces. Anyway, my family packed my bags for me, took me to the airport, put me on the plane for Bangkok and just prayed that I would arrive safely. When I landed at Bangkok airport a taxi was waiting for me and took me directly to the monastery.

When I arrived at Thamkrabok the monks took my bags and removed all the drugs, including the prescription drugs. In this place you go cold turkey and everything had to be stopped, including legal and prescription drugs. It's a massive detox. I was on a hell of a lot of stuff at that time so my detox was pretty fucking crazy. I only got a couple of hours' sleep here and there in the first 20 days. Twenty days into the program I managed my first 3-hour sleep, 3 consecutive hours. Think about it, I was coming off heroin, alcohol, dhaperazine – that one was flowing in my blood – coming off the sleepers and more. Effexor took the longest to get rid of because I was still getting electric shocks off that drug even after 13 days. That's what I'm on now. It's an antidepressant. I took one this morning because if I didn't take it I would be feeling strange and fuzzy and like my arms and legs would be twitching and that's just what the withdrawal symptoms of one drug are like. Can you imagine the state I was in at Thamkrabok, coming off loads of drugs all at once? It's supposed to be 5 days of vomiting to purge the drugs from the system but I was still puking after 13 days. That's how you detox, you vomit it all out so it's known as the vomiting monastery. Every day at about 4pm is vomit time. The monks line you up in front of a gulley next to a bucket of water. You have an empty shot glass and the medicine man comes round with a bucket which contains a mixture of herbs. It's a brown, sloppy mixture that you have to drink while they watch you. It's made from 108 different herbs and you have to drink it with the entire bucket of water. It's hard trying to vomit.

Everybody shares the same gulley. The monks kept saying, "Drink more water, drink more water" because you have to spew up the herbs and the more water you drink the easier it is to be sick. At least that's what they say but I tell you it was horrible, really horrible. There we all were, lined up at the gulley spewing our guts out. All sorts of people, girls as well as guys, and many nationalities but our common ground was addiction and the fact that we had all found our way to this very unusual place.

Life at the monastery isn't a walk in the park. At 4:30am the bell rings and we have to get up. I don't know why they ring the bell so early. I mean we were all feeling dreadful because we were all in the middle of our detox. Added to that discomfort was the dreadful itching I was experiencing because I had been bitten to pieces by mosquitoes. There were mosquito nets but we still got bitten. Men and women slept in separate rooms in a dormitory, average of about 12 or 13 men and slightly less women. They kept the Westerners separate from the Thai addicts. The women got locked in at night and a monk slept outside their door. Maybe there was about 35 Thai men and 25 women in a separate dorm. We all slept in an area of the monastery called the Hey.

Most of the Thais in there were on a drug called yaba which is like crystal meth. It's the big thing in Thailand apparently. They can make it very cheap by diluting it with thinners that really fucks up people's heads. It was originally manufactured by the Nazis to help keep their troops awake for days but now it's more widespread than heroin in Thailand. Lots of people in the Hey were alcoholics too. There was a real thin old guy who must have been in his 80s. I felt really sorry for him when he was spewing. I stayed with the monks for 30 days, then returned home. I stayed clean and sober for 13 months.

Arriving back in Ireland I knew I needed some support so I contacted an aftercare center and joined the support group. After a year I had to pinch myself that I was still clean. I knew it was amazing I had done that. But then I made the big mistake of getting back with my ex-girlfriend. As soon as I got back with her we got into the same old patterns. It was a messed-up relationship but even so, we ended up moving in together. We were endlessly at war. I was totally focused on her and not much else. It was the emotional stuff that I couldn't handle. At that time I hadn't heard of codependency within relationships but looking back I can see how this was a classic codependent relationship. One day I said to her "One of us is going to end up abusing" and I knew it would be me. I didn't tell her it would be me but I knew I was going to use, I just knew it. And I was right because not long after that we had a huge row just before I went off to aftercare. I was sitting in the aftercare group and suddenly I just got up and left without saying a word and ran to the car and went out and drove into town and scored some heroin. I was disgusted with myself. So there I was – I was using again, straight back into my old pattern. This time I ended up on methadone which is a substitute for heroin. It was legal, prescribed by the doctor.

So many of my friends have died since Greg died. Like there were two friends of mine that used to go to the same methadone clinic as me. One day they handed us out a leaflet warning us about some dodgy valium tablets that were being sold on the streets. A few people had died from them in a nearby town. The next day my mates had these valium and offered some to me but I said "I'm not taking them." They were a strange color so I suspected they were the dodgy ones. I told them about the warning leaflet but they ignored me and took them. This was on a Sunday.

Ed died on the Monday. He was found dead in his bed. William died on the Wednesday. He too was found dead in his bed. Both of them were in their 30s, not old. I found that really freaky. How had I found the strength to say no to those valium when I was used to taking anything that was on offer? I keep telling myself that there has to be a reason for me still being here.

So I stayed on the methadone and eventually I managed to get a place in a center that does a medical detox. It's a fantastic place, the only available medical detox in Ireland. It took me 8 months to get in there. You have to give four clear urine samples for a week to be able to get in so my counselor said "Do a couple of samples today because they'll be clear today and count it as two separate tests" and he pulled some strings for me to get me in. I'm so grateful to him. That guy had faith in me. It was him who managed to get me to sleep in a bed. I was so used to sleeping in small spaces that I've got a really bad back. On the streets I slept in doorways and in the squat I used to sleep on a two-seater couch with wooden arms so I was used to being bent up like a fetus. I found it impossible to make the adjustment from sleeping on the couch to sleeping in the bed. I couldn't spread my body out. And I needed the TV on in the background to be able to get to sleep. When he first met me this counselor said "How can we help him, what can we do with him? He's too young to die but that's what's happening, he's going to die…"

I was in there for 7 weeks, not cold turkey but down to 50ml of methadone and 40g of valium. They take you down gradually. Each morning they give you a bit less. To be honest, I was so sick in there that they had to bring the doctor in several times. I was anemic and my eyes were jet black. They're called raccoon eyes, all black underneath. They said that when I first came in they thought I had died when they found me lying on the couch. I looked so ill that I was like a corpse. Physically I was in bits because of my lifestyle. I was bloated up to 14 and a half stone from the methadone. I was huge. I lost 2 stone inside there. I started eating veggies and healthy food and the weight fell off. The weight loss was helped by the amount of sweat I was losing. I was getting through more than a dozen shirts a day through sweating. Each time I changed my shirt it got soaked through in less than an hour.

One day I was so incredibly ill that I said to them "Get me a syringe and fill it. I can't stay here and I can't go out and use so I might as well die." They were really good though. They just stayed and talked to me until that feeling passed. I was glad I stuck with the detox because looking back I can see the desperation I was feeling was just in my head. Anyway, I came out of there, spent 2 months with my mum and dad and then came out here to New Life. I had heard about this place when I was in Thamkrabok. A guy called Vince Cullen had come to visit the monks while I was in there doing my detox and he walked in with a bucket of KFC, loads of fried chicken and chips. I didn't know him but we all thought 'Nice one, man' and we became friends on Facebook so that's how I kept in contact with him. He was fantastic, even when I was back using. It was great to have support like that. He told me about New Life. He kept saying that if I could get clean I could get into here. The monastery had detoxed me and dealt with the physical symptoms of addiction but had not dealt with the root causes.

Being at New Life has been really eye-opening. I have changed since I got here. I find it difficult to put my finger on exactly what the change has been and how I have managed to make that change. Is it community? Is it my head getting better? It's hard to say.

It hasn't been easy. It was particularly hard when I first arrived. I was so used to isolating myself that I found it really difficult talking to people and suddenly there I am surrounded by people all the time. I was freaked out by that. My first 10 days I was ready to bolt out of the door but now I'm starting to really get into it. I'm realizing why I'm here. I'm here for myself. Everything is starting to fall into place. Here you get counseling, workshops, meditation, yoga, good food, working in the fields and such like. There's a good balance between work, self-awareness and free time. And then there are the members of the community. They're so supportive of each other. There have been challenges and there still are but I keep telling myself that each challenge makes me stronger, like that song: 'What doesn't kill you makes you stronger.'

Recently the resident nun gave me a book to read: *When Things Fall Apart* by Pema Chödrön. The author's husband told Pema that she was one of the bravest people he knew. She said, "Why?" and he replied, "Because you are a coward, but you do things anyway." That put things in my head, that I'm not the only one who is a coward and who is afraid to face things. In here, I put myself outside my comfort zone constantly, and I'm actually benefiting from it. It's not always an easy process but as one of my life coaches puts it: "Short-term pain for long-term gain." I used to live my life the other way around.

It's been a waste of a life to be honest. My mum said that most of the time she had to assume I was dead because that's the only way she could cope. So I reckon it's time for me to get my act together and grow up for her sake as much as my own. I should have been dead many times but I keep feeling that I have been kept alive for a purpose. The biggest thing, the most important thing is what goes on inside us, not what's going on outside. I have the power to change what goes on inside me. Looking at emotions in meditation and accepting them actually takes the power out of them. That's the thing I'm learning here.

Gretel's Story

I'm German and I'm 27 years old and I came to the New Life Foundation as a volunteer. I was traveling around Thailand on my own and I was looking for somewhere to stay, ideally a yoga and meditation retreat. I checked out all the ones I could find in southern Thailand around the islands and so on but they just seemed superficial to me. Then, on one of the volunteer websites – either Workaway or Wwoof – I saw that this place was looking for volunteers. I didn't know much about it, only that it was mostly self-sufficient and had farming and yoga and meditation. For some reason I just felt really drawn to this place. By that point I had already traveled around the north of Thailand so part of me was reluctant to return to the area I had already visited. I really would have preferred to see a different part of the country but the instinctive feeling to head for New Life was so strong that I just had to come. So I did.

I never checked out their website before coming here. I simply saw the advert on Workaway and followed my gut instinct. At that time I didn't know about all the other stuff that goes on here. I came as a volunteer but as soon as I arrived I became very ill and spent a lot of time in bed. It seemed to me as if I was reacting to something. It started with my eyes. They got really bloodshot and sore and then my stomach started playing up. Everyone was very understanding and they let me stay in bed to recover. I felt bad that I had come as a volunteer but I couldn't work. I simply couldn't understand why I was so unwell.

While I was lying in bed I had plenty of time to think and to reflect on things. It was as if my body had gone into illness in order to force me to stop and take stock of my life. I decided to have some life coaching as there are a few life coaches at New Life and they're available for sessions throughout the week. Also, I'm really interested in the Enneagram and some of the therapists here use that in their work so I decided to explore that. So I studied that and gained so much from it. It really helped me to understand myself. I'm a 9 and when I learned about being a number 9, all sorts of things fell into place for me because a 9 is a peacemaker and that's always what I'm striving for, peace.

After a few counseling sessions, several of the life coaches suggested that I could try joining the residents' program rather than working as a volunteer. I was very resistant to it. I thought 'No, I don't need this, I'm fine, I have dealt with all my problems.' But then one of the other volunteers said "Look, you have the opportunity to look deep into yourself. How often does an opportunity like that arise? So why not do it?" I thought she was right and I knew I could always change back to being a volunteer if I changed my mind and that's how I moved onto the residents' program.

The residents' program is fantastic because it combines yoga, meditation, working mindfully within the community, sessions with the life coaches and group workshops. I actually prefer one-to-one therapy because I feel more comfortable with that but looking back I can see the huge benefits of the group sharing. The group work was really challenging at first but once I allowed myself to open up it was so freeing. It was powerful and beautiful. You just put it out there with no mask, no façade, saying, 'This is me, take it or leave it.' I don't think I had ever done that before in my entire life. I had always been concerned with what other people thought of me and how they would judge me.

I was raised as Christian evangelist but it never did anything for me. I'm very open to spirituality but I'm not really religious. My parents weren't that religious but they sent me to be confirmed because they had been married in church so they thought it would be nice if we could get married in church too. But I never married Brad although I lived with him.

I met Brad at the age of 14. He was 7 years older than me. He was at college with my brother, studying the same subjects. One day he was standing at my parents' door waiting for my brother. Our eyes locked and that was it. As soon as I saw him I just fell head over heels in love with him. I truly believe in love at first sight and I'm so grateful that I have had a chance to experience such love. At first we were just friends because he already had a girlfriend. We would spend hours just chatting and enjoying each other's company and that went on for about 2 years before we started kissing. Finally when I was 16 he split up from his girlfriend and we got together. We moved in together when I turned 18. Before that we spent a lot of time together at his place because he shared a flat with his sister. His family was very close and family orientated. They really took me into their home and their hearts. I felt like their daughter. Their home was so unlike the home that I had come from. My parents never communicated with me and hardly ever hugged me. That's because they were always so busy working on the farm. It was an eye-opening experience for me to see how another family operated. My family didn't really talk but his family talked about absolutely everything in the smallest detail.

My grandmother – my dad's mother – lived with us and my mum's mum lived nearby. She more or less raised us and I'm really close to her, more so than to my mother. My grandmother was affectionate. Actually my mum did touch me, stroke my back and so on when I was watching TV but it felt awkward, not so much as a child but certainly as I got older. It was as if there was a distance between us. I was a real stroppy teenager.

Nobody understood me! My dad didn't get involved because I don't think he knew what to do.

I remember a really memorable and significant incident when I was a very young child. I saw my mum and dad outside the barn door in their working clothes kissing each other like mad and me and my brother stood watching them. Very soon after that my dad started having affairs. My mum knew about this but I think she thought they would be able to work things out. I remember seeing Mum crying in the bedroom and she was in pieces and then they started having separate bedrooms. But nobody ever explained to me what was going on. All the time I was wondering what had happened. I couldn't understand: 'What has happened to Mum and Dad? Why is this woman always here sitting on the sofa snuggling up to my dad while my mum is sitting on the armchair?' My mum was trying to be tolerant because she didn't want to lose him so she actually allowed this woman into our home.

She only opened up about this quite recently. She explained to me that my dad just needed some sort of vitality in his life and maybe it was just a phase and so my mum let it happen. She didn't have the strength to walk away because she loved him so much. She didn't want to break up the family because of the children too. Having the farm she had no life of her own because it was always work, work, work from morning until night. Even sometimes during the night too!

Mum tried to be friends with this woman because the relationship that she had with my father wasn't short-lived. It went on for years. It was very strange. My dad would meet up with this woman and her children and we were told that we had to play together so they could go and snuggle together and it all felt really awkward. I would ask "Why isn't Mum coming with us?" but that question was never really answered. Dad said the woman was just a friend and we should like her because she's a nice woman. Sometimes she came to our house and sometimes we went to her house and we would often see them kissing. It was very puzzling for a child to see that on a regular basis. In the end my parents ended up getting divorced. They divorced when I was 20.

I was still with Brad when they divorced, living in Germany, but soon after the divorce we moved to England together. It was his idea. He was always full of crazy ideas. We often spoke about going to live abroad but more like a fantasy than a reality. I never thought we actually would go even though the idea of it sounded like fun. But Brad was Brad and he was a very spontaneous sort of person. One Monday he went to work and at the end of the day he came back and said he'd quit his job and he said "I'm moving to England, do you want to come?"

At the time I was working as a hairdresser and the job was okay but nothing special so I thought, 'Why not?' We moved in with Brad's brother and his English girlfriend. They lived in the north of England. I soon found work as a hairdresser in the town. Brad was a car mechanic so he found work easily too.

We lived together for 6 months with his brother and girlfriend but then we started to clash and there was a bad atmosphere in the house. We decided we'd be better off and happier if we could find our own place so we found a house to rent nearby. It was lovely, just the two of us in our own place. I was 21 at this time.

We lived happily there for four and a half years, close to the city center and all the pubs and clubs. We had a nice group of friends and my hairdressing career began to take off. I was offered jobs for TV, films and fashion shows. It was a whole new world for me and it was exactly what I had wanted to do. In England I had finally found what I was looking for work-wise. By this time Brad was 33 and I was 26. Because of the age gap I think he was a bit of a father figure.

Then his brother split up with his girlfriend. They had been together for 10 years so it was a bit of a shock for everyone. After that we decided to move back in with his brother. The idea was to join in with the mortgage so that we could own the house together. The brother was spending a lot of time in Germany so we often had the house to ourselves. It was great to be in a place that belonged to us. We could really start to make it a home. We had big plans and after 3 months we had already started knocking down walls and renovating the place. Life was good and the future looked bright.

For the first time since we met I felt ready to make the commitment. I felt it so strongly, that it was the right thing to do, to commit to him 100%. He had just been waiting for me to reach that point. I guess my parents' divorce had made me reluctant to commit. Also the fact that he was my first boyfriend ever. I had only ever been with him so I didn't have much experience. But I loved him and wanted to be with him and so I decided to commit.

The morning of his death was weird because I was supposed to drive him to work that day but then he decided that he would go on the motorbike. That morning there was some tension between us and we started niggling and I said "I don't want to fall out with you." I said "It's not worth arguing about anything because we love each other so let's stop. Don't go to work feeling bad." His mum had always said to me to treat each goodbye as if it was the last one, that no fight is worth it. He blew me a kiss as he left. How could I possibly have guessed that this would be our last goodbye?

It wasn't raining. In fact it was a beautiful day. We think that he was going too fast and he misjudged the bend. There was another car involved. To this day we don't know the exact details of the accident. The other car involved was a Porsche but the driver didn't turn up for the inquest. We could have had a private investigation but I decided not to go down that route, partly because it's too painful, but really it won't bring him back, so what is the point? That driver saw somebody die and he will be carrying that memory for ever.

Anyway, let me tell you about that day. I got home from work and started cooking the evening meal. As I was cooking I was talking to my friend in Germany on the phone and I remember saying to her "God, I wish he wouldn't do this, coming home so late without letting me know. All he has to do is send me a text because he knows I worry if he's late." As a mechanic he was sometimes late because he had jobs to finish before he could leave work. I had just put the phone down when I saw a police car driving down my road. I knew they were coming for me. I just knew. I sensed it. And I was right. They knocked on my door and when I opened it they said, "I'm sorry but there has been an accident, a motorbike accident..."

But even though they said those words, still you don't believe it. I simply couldn't believe it. I thought, 'This can't be right, they must have got the wrong person. This can't be happening. He must be still in hospital, injured but still able to speak to me and tell me what happened. He can't just be gone. It's not possible. They have made a mistake. He was wearing a helmet and he had all the right gear so he can't have been killed.'

But they hadn't made a mistake. The nightmare was true.

I went into shock. I had some good friends and the police waited for them to arrive and made sure that I had their support before they left the house.

Even talking about that dreadful day still affects me. I'm shaking now so it's still in my body. However, it doesn't consume me anymore, not like it used to. It doesn't take control over me these days. In the past I would lose complete control of my body. I wouldn't be able to breathe. I wouldn't be able to see or hear. It sounds incredible but it's true. I would just completely blank out.

Now while I am talking about it my legs are shaking like crazy and my heart is beating really fast but it's not as bad as it was. I used to get a feeling like a thousand razor blades in my throat but that doesn't happen now. Actually this is the first time it hasn't happened. Maybe that's because I did some trauma release work here at New Life. It's called TRE. It releases trauma that is caught at the cellular level.

I breathe into my belly and that helps, not to fight the sensations that arise in my body but to breathe through them. Not to suppress them but to try and flow through those feelings with the breath.

I think that sudden death is the most difficult sort of death to deal with. It's like the rug is taken from under you. From one second to the next your life can just change and be turned completely upside down. I see now that the future is just an illusion. It doesn't exist except in your mind.

The day after he died I flew back to Germany. I just wanted to be with his family. My mum came to stay with them too and she stayed for weeks because she had been brought into his family too. It felt safe and supportive being there. The day I arrived in Germany the doctor came and gave me an injection to calm me down. He also gave me some antidepressants and some sleeping tablets to help me to sleep. Brad's sister said, "No, don't have it. You need to go through the grieving process. It's much better to deal with the emotions when they arise instead of numbing out the pain."

In retrospect I wish I hadn't done that because all it did was delay my recovery. It took me over 3 years to deal with what had happened. I took the medication for about 3 months. I kind of said that I didn't want the drugs but I didn't have the strength to say no. I needed help and support.

I don't remember much about those early days. I do remember one day when I completely freaked and I started crying and screaming, screaming his name in utter grief and pain and that frightened them and again they called the doctor because they felt so helpless, they didn't know what to do with me. What they didn't understand is that this is exactly what I needed to do, I just needed to scream Brad's name out to get rid of those feelings, to scream and scream until I was emptied of pain. Maybe those razor blades I felt in my throat were caused by my not being allowed to scream out in pain, emotional pain, the pain of loss and grief and helplessness. Instead I was tranquilized by the medicine and all of those feelings were suppressed.

I wish I'd said, 'I don't want all these tablets and injections' but the thing is that the people around me cared for me and they were only trying to help me. They couldn't bear to see and hear me in such pain.

It would have been useful and helpful to have had people around me who knew what was best for me. They could have stepped up on my behalf to say, 'No, let her go through the grief, it'll be better in the long run.' But I don't blame anybody for the decisions that were taken. People were just trying their best to help me and they didn't know what was best for me in the long run. I do know now that if anyone I knew had to go through what I have gone through, I would tell them not to take any medication if possible.

I have seen so many beautiful signs since Brad's death, from rainbows to bees. It was the hottest summer in Germany after he died. This bee kept annoying me. Every day he came and buzzed around my food as I tried to eat. This bee was just the same as Brad because he used to tease me.

Then when I went to choose the place for his grave there was this plant that kept getting trapped in my trousers, so much so that I couldn't move. It was a space right on the top of a hill so I knew that was Brad's resting place.

I wish I'd written down all the signs because they were so incredible. It confirmed to me that there was life after this life.

The year after he died I passed my motorbike license test. People might think I'm crazy to do that but doing it brought me closer to him and his memory. And it has given me such freedom because now I can hire a bike anywhere I go.

Eventually, after 3 months in Germany I plucked up the courage to go back to England. Living in England had been a joint choice, *our* choice. I went back to the house that we had lived in and the brother's ex-girlfriend had sorted the house out and cleared away his belongings because she didn't want me to come home and find his washing in the laundry basket and stuff like that. She had sorted it out and put it into boxes. That was so thoughtful, she's like an angel. She also supported her ex-boyfriend through the loss of his brother despite her own pain.

I can't remember if I went back to England alone or not which is strange. I guess that memory is still blocked. But I do remember getting on the train in Germany and the ticket had exactly the same number as the car that he had when we first met. His number plate was DAN D 259 and I was sitting in seat DAN D 259. I had even made his number plate my password on my school computer so to see it appearing as I traveled back to our former home in England was an incredible coincidence. I felt as if he was with me on that journey.

I haven't had any other relationships since he died. I haven't felt ready. In fact, since he died I have lived a bit of a reckless life. My coping strategy isn't addiction because I have this natural ability to numb myself out completely. I had been living in this numbed-out state for a long time. I tried to spend my time getting on with my life and having fun but all those unprocessed feelings were still inside me, eating away at my insides. I kept on working. In fact I became a bit of a workaholic because that was a way to avoid dealing with my 'stuff'. Stuff is a good word to use because that is what had happened to the feelings and emotions. They were stuffed inside me.

I couldn't talk about his death for years. The lid first started to come off last year when I decided I wanted to start traveling. This idea has always been there in the background but when Brad was alive I wouldn't have had the confidence to leave him and go traveling. I was very insecure and I was afraid that he might have left me or met somebody else while I was away. I was needy but being without him I gradually learned that I was able to do things on my own. Don't forget, he had been in my life since the age of 14. I was so young when I met him.

Anyway, I started by going away for short city breaks, just for a night or two. Once I got used to doing that I came up with the idea of going traveling for 6 weeks. Then I thought maybe 3 months. In the end I thought 'Screw this, I'm going to go traveling without a time limit!'

I can choose my own path, for myself, see where life takes me. I feel really blessed to have had that love in my life so now I'm continuing on my own path. I'm now a nomad. I have no home. His brother bought out my share of the house and I have savings from my former manic work life which will allow me to travel for quite a while.

You know sometimes really terrible things happen but good can come out of the tragedy. I'm not saying it was a good thing that he died but so much positivity has blossomed out of such an awful incident. I finally got my dad back, got everything I need from him and my brother. What happened is that my brother and my dad drove through Europe to pick up my stuff from the English house for me. It was a road trip and while we were traveling together we had many intense conversations. It bonded us all for the first time ever. It has changed their lives too because now we have an honesty, an openness between us. I cleared up so much from my childhood. Once that lid came off all sorts of stuff began to come out.

I have learned so much about myself here at New Life. The main thing I have learned is that we are all looking for love but all we need to do is to break down the barriers that we build against it. The love is already there. I am now open to love and I'm not going to deny myself love. Despite the pain of the loss that I have experienced, I know that my blocks have been released so now I can love again.

Liam's Story

I was born by caesarian section 10 years after my brother. I'm the youngest of four children. I do sometimes wonder whether I was meant to be here, whether I should have been born at all. Mum had been advised not to have any more children after the third one and she was almost 40 when she had me. I remember my older brother saying to me:

One child is a necessity,
Two is a luxury,
Three is a mistake,
Four is a disaster.

That was humiliating. It kind of made a deep impression on me.

I'm quite dark-skinned and when Mum came round after the caesarian and I was brought to her she said "That's not my baby. He's black. I haven't got a black baby." Maybe it was the anesthetic wearing off that made her say that or maybe she has a thing about dark skin. Mum has quite dark skin. My gran (my mum's mum) had dark skin too and she even tried to bleach my mum's skin when she was a child.

After I was born my mum was allowed to stay in hospital for longer than normal. I think the doctors could see that my dad wasn't the most caring and compassionate person in the world and she needed looking after. Despite her initial rejection of me, I guess I must have bonded with my mum during those few days in hospital because I do feel bonded with her. I breastfed for quite a long time. I was still breastfeeding after I learned to speak because I have been told that I called her boobs 'booze'. "I want booze" I used to say, a bit ironic really, considering my later alcoholism!

My dad worked away quite often. He was a telecommunications expert and could be away for months at a time. I remember saying to Mum that I had forgotten what he looked like and I had to ask to see photos of him. Mum told me recently that he had been jilted not that long before they got married. Dad could never talk to me about that kind of stuff but I'm sure that it must have had an effect on his confidence.

Both sides of my family are descended from farm workers, living off the land, typical Irish families. My mum came from a very staunch Irish Catholic background. Her father was a very well-read man and very wise. It is said that Ireland is a land of saints and scholars and from my experience that is a true analysis. It's not necessary to have a formal education to be educated. My granddad was self-taught but no less scholarly because of it.

Dad was oldest of 11 kids because birth control was a no-no if you were Catholic. Dad won't talk about his father. He talks about his uncle who was a priest but I have never once heard him talk about my grandfather. To this day I don't know why and it's not the sort of question I could ask him. We don't have that sort of relationship.

Dad. What can I say about him? He can be very charming but there is another side to him. He's a Jekyll and Hyde character. I would say he has a personality disorder. I can just look at him and see which personality he is in, the negative or the positive. When he is negative he has a moody, dark presence which is very unpleasant. He can be callous, unsympathetic, cruel, selfish and verbally unkind. He never hit my mum but he was abusive verbally towards her. He hit his kids though, with his big strong hands that were like shovels. He would rage out of control and it was scary. When he lost it he beat us like a mad man. There was no love in him. He seemed to use us as a release for his own anger and frustration. I think there was something (forgive me for saying it) perverted about the way he hit us. It was the look on his face when he did it. He really went wild. It's one thing to be disciplined but another thing entirely to be physically abused with violence. I can accept discipline if it is done with love and

I'm sure that is possible, but he did it with no love.

Mum was quiet, timid and completely overawed by him, a meek and mild country girl. She couldn't control his moods. He did exactly what he wanted and always got his own way. She would rather sweep things under the carpet than deal with them. She has found a bit more confidence now but while I was growing up she was a real martyr looking after four kids on her own while Dad was away and totally under his thumb when he was home. When I see old photos of my mum I can see how ill and run-down she was at that time. She was really thin, very depressed and having to take medication to help her to sleep. Her weight really plummeted and she was in a very bad state but my dad didn't seem to notice it. He was obsessed with his work. That's all he did: work, work, work.

She had a very strong faith, strongly Catholic. We all went to church and became fully indoctrinated. I didn't mind going because we all went together as a family, the whole lot of us. Mum and Dad are still very involved in the church. I haven't been to church for a long time but my parents actually hand out the host these days. I quite liked saying my prayers to God and Jesus as a child. I had Holy Communion and was even an altar boy for a while. I stopped going to church when I was a teenager.

The first mystical experience was when I was about 4 or 5 years old and I looked in the mirror on the wardrobe and said, "Who am I?" That moment of looking into my own eyes was very strong. I looked at my eyes and my eyes looked back at me. Why did I do that at such a young age? Something happened there. I felt something and the moment remains in my memory very clearly. From then on I knew that my life was going to be different to other people's lives. I never heard anybody else talking about experiences like the one that I had. My mum's mum was said to be very psychic. There are parts of Ireland that are famous for its seers and I was told that I have the gift. I just know it's true. It's what I was born with. So from a young age I have

46

lived with the knowledge that I was different. As I got into my teenage years I started having premonitions and precognitive dreams. I would go into a kind of sleep – it's hard to explain – but I would hear an echo in my head as if I was going into the core of the universe. I couldn't talk to my friends about this. I mean it's not the sort of thing you chat about with your 13-year-old buddies, is it? I never told my parents about any of this either. I kept it all hidden.

I was always very popular at school when I was young. I was good at sport, had girlfriends, my grades were reasonable and life was okay. When I look back I saw that it all started to change when I got into solvent abuse, mostly using aerosol. I was using solvents to try and cope with all the weird things that were happening, all the psychic stuff. Each time something cosmic happened I thought 'Do some more aerosol.' I wanted these strange things to stop.

Aerosol is inhaled and when you breathe it, it feels like a coldness going down inside you. Taking this stuff worked in that it would knock me out but the solvent really triggered something bad in me. It changed me for the worse. I was doing cannabis as well even though I was only 13 years old but cannabis is harder to get hold of at that age. Solvents are easy to get hold of and they're an easy high but very dangerous and they are addictive too. I grew out of that and moved on to LSD and speed, then ecstasy, then cocaine and of course all the time there was alcohol. Whenever I could get hold of alcohol I drank.

I was caught shoplifting when I was 13. I did it for a dare. I didn't want the things I was stealing, it was more for the thrill of it but then I was caught stealing a music tape. It was awful, the hand on the shoulder, your heart sinks, they call home and of course Dad was told about it. He hit me hard for it. I knew it was wrong but I was doing it to fit in, to be one of the gang. There was a lot of peer pressure and really it was just a rite of passage but Mum was afraid that I was going off the rails and she didn't know how to discipline me so she told my dad and let him dish out the discipline. I told her that my dad might fire the bullets but she was the one who loaded the gun because she didn't discipline me, she left it up to him. He would punish me emotionally, physically and psychologically. I don't think she understood the impact this was having on me. It was deeply upsetting. I was helpless. There was nothing I could do to defend myself. It was unfair.

By the time I left home at the age of 19 to go to university I already had a deeply established pattern of drug and alcohol abuse and a history of depression. The first time I experienced depression was when I was 16. I had left school and gone to college to study for A-levels. I didn't know what was happening to me. I didn't know what depression was. I just knew that I felt out of place, that something wasn't right. At college I was out of my comfort zone. I had an inferiority complex and I was taking loads of drugs because they were freely available. I was struck down with depression and became withdrawn and isolated. I changed. My personality changed. I didn't go to the doctor. Even my mum who is a nurse didn't suggest seeing the doctor. So I started doing even more drugs and alcohol as a way of coping but clearly it was making it worse. I had a total loss of confidence. Any confidence I had felt as I was growing up all evaporated.

On my 17th birthday I was in the midst of this depression and I went out with my mates. One of them was a dealer and he had these ecstasy tablets with some ketamine in them. I took four of them which is far too many. It's a dangerous amount. I ended up at the club with my eyes rolling. I couldn't even stand, never mind walk, so much so that I fell down a long flight of stairs. It was crazy. I could have died but that's the way I was – I was prone to excess, no limits, I didn't know when to stop. I don't seem to possess that self-limiting gene. I didn't get chucked out of the club because my mate was the bouncer but I do resent my drug dealer friend a bit. He shouldn't have sold me so many tablets.

I had wanted to do a degree in psychology at university but I failed the first year so I changed to a sociology degree instead. I was put into emergency accommodation when I arrived because there weren't enough spaces in hall. It was a tower block with prostitutes and druggies around. The guy I was supposed to be sharing with didn't turn up and I was going nuts because I was there all on my own. I just sat in my room taking drugs and getting more and more paranoid and depressed.

Mostly I was smoking cannabis. That drug is so bad for causing paranoia. If you have the slightest tendency towards it then cannabis will blow it up out of all proportion. I became so paranoid it was unbelievable. I wouldn't open the door to anyone because I thought that whoever was knocking wanted to kill me. I wouldn't even go near the front door in case someone put an umbrella through the door with poison on the end of it. I still remember when a Hungarian spy was killed that way on London Bridge. That happened on my birthday which is maybe why it made such an impression on me.

Being at university triggered my depression again. I got by for a while in university but then I began flunking it. It was a struggle and I actually decided to use the student counseling service. I only went once. The body language of the woman... she just sat there... I don't know... I just never went back. She looked as if she wasn't interested in me.

Soon I was moved into better accommodation and I began to make some friends. Being at uni there was drink and drugs everywhere, so easy to get hold of stuff. We had drinking games and happy hour. The very first night I went out with some other students I ended up in hospital. There were these big buckets of alcohol and you could drink as much as you wanted. I had no limits. I don't know when to stop. I don't have that ability to regulate my drinking so I just got hammered and I blacked out. I woke up in hospital. I didn't know where I was or what had happened but I just laughed it off.

Those drinking games are dangerous. The following year a student died from alcohol poisoning playing the bucket game. They should be banned.

Next time I went out with them I got into a fight. The beer was so cheap you could just drink loads so once again I was hammered. I laid into some guy and punched him in the face so hard that he ended up in hospital for 2 weeks but I was so drunk I didn't even realize what I had done. The bouncers came and I was thrown onto the pavement. His mates beat me up and I was walking around college with two black eyes.

The students I was hanging out with drank so much and whenever I drank I became violent and aggressive. That was the effect that alcohol had on my behavior. Then I got into the druggies group which was better for me. The pot didn't make me aggressive and so I got more into drugs. I did a lot of partying, taking ecstasy and snorting cocaine. I mostly took ecstasy at the weekend, starting with one but as it goes on you need more and more as if you build up a tolerance for it. It used to be that one pill would last 8 to 10 hours but soon I needed two pills, then three. Even though I was taking all these drugs I was still drinking quite heavily.

I can't remember when I first went to a doctor with my depression. Sometime in my early 20s I guess and they prescribed Prozac. I wasn't fully engaged in taking these drugs because I didn't really accept that I had a problem. I knew it wasn't right the way I was feeling. Even my mum wasn't saying anything. She was doing her 'sweep it under the carpet' act, like if we don't talk about it, it won't be real. What I needed was for Mum to say 'You're depressed and this is what we need to do.' Instead she said "Oh, it's a phase you're going through. You'll bounce out of it."

It was 'snap out of it', that kind of mentality. There was a part of me that didn't really mind her taking that attitude because I didn't want to be thought of as someone with a mental illness. I took a few of the Prozac but never went back for more. I actually snorted them to get a hit but nothing happened so I thought 'These things don't bloody work.' I was under the impression they'd given me a placebo.

My depression would come in waves. I used illegal drugs and alcohol to self-medicate. I smoked skunk which is really strong cannabis but it wasn't good for my mind. Every 5 years I thought I was turning a corner but then when I was 34 I just was drinking a lot, taking cocaine, feeling really depressed and not knowing what was going on. It was at about this age that the depression really set in. This time the wave came and wouldn't go away and I knew I had to do something about it. I was blacking out quite frequently, waking up in all sorts of places, no idea where I was, where I had been or where I was going. People around me could see I was right off the rails and they said I needed to stop and seek some help. I did stop drinking for a while but at the same time I withdrew from people. My dry periods would last a few weeks. One of the reasons I had to stop drinking was because my hangovers were getting so bad. So I would stop for a few weeks and then when I felt a bit better I would go out binging again. I would have a massive binge, then I'd stop for a while to detox, then go on a binge again. I did tend to binge rather than drink a smaller amount on a regular basis. I started getting arrested, banned from pubs, being charged with public disorder offenses and regularly ending up in hospital or a police cell.

My life was chaos but I didn't know how to stop the roller coaster. I wanted to get off. I wanted to take control of my addictions but I lacked the ability to do that. I started taking prescription drugs again and I took tablets I got off the internet. I was taking Ritalin and diazepam but nothing was changing.

Then I was called up for jury service and that was the last straw. I just couldn't handle it. I was in no fit state to be a member of a jury. It was a sexual assault case. I knew from day one it would be a hung jury. I'm still psychic despite all my attempts to keep a lid on all that. It's always there just under the surface. I was proved right as the jury was hung. I couldn't take the stress, this 'I was right and they were wrong.' I became very indignant within myself. I told the court that I was stressed and they said I had to get a doctor's note. That's what got me back to the doctor. I knew that CBT was available and the doctor agreed that would be the best treatment for me, rather than prescription drugs. It was good. It helped me to manage my moods and it demonstrated to me how distorted my thought forms were but although CBT was really helpful, it never gave me the answers from deep inside me. So it helped me to some extent but didn't deal with my true issue which is addiction.

It was after Claire died that things came to a head. I had known Claire all my life. I used to spend time at her house and her at mine. She was born the day before me. We went to different schools but I met up with her after school and also at college. We took drugs together. I didn't know that she was an alcoholic. Nobody knew. She was hiding it from me. We would go out drinking together but what I didn't realize was that she would drink before and after we went out. One night we did acid together and she asked me to walk her home and I said no. Then she tried kissing me and I didn't respond because it didn't feel right. I felt guilty that I hadn't taken my opportunity of having a relationship with her. Maybe I could have helped her but it would have felt a bit incestuous because she felt like family to me.

She died just a few months ago. Her liver was weak and had packed up from doing too much alcohol. She had overdosed on drink and drugs. When I heard about her death it affected me very deeply.

One of the last times I had a drink I was with some friends and they hadn't heard about her death and one guy said "Oh well, she was an alcoholic" in such a dismissive way. That was a cruel thing to say. I got horribly drunk that day, maybe because of that. I had no lunch, drank strong lager and gin and tonics and I remember nothing after 6pm. Apparently I was getting rowdy and asking everyone for cocaine. I was asked to leave the bar so I tried to get over the fence – I wanted to get out without having to walk through the pub. I could have fallen and died. One of my brother's friends died falling off a marquee when he was drunk. I have been very stupid but very lucky, like I have been kept alive.

Claire's death was what made me make the commitment to deal with my alcoholism and stop. It's as if I was pushing myself to crisis point, like I had to hit rock bottom before I could deal with it. It took a while to hit rock bottom but that was the day I did.

I turned to my doctor for help and it was suggested that I had one-to-one counseling but I found the one-to-one sessions far too intense. However, the counselor told me about the SADAS group. It's a charity and they offer drug and alcohol counseling. I contacted them and said, "I want to control my drinking but you probably want me to abstain before I can come along to the group" and they said, "No, we don't require that." I was really glad about that as I was incapable of stopping so I went along. This was the first time in my life that I met people who understood me. When we shared within the group I heard other people speak and we all had experienced similar things. Despite our background etc. there were common threads with all our stories. I did their 12-week course and I felt I had done well by completing it. After that I knew I needed a new challenge and I told them I was going to Thailand. I had stopped working some months earlier so I was free to travel. I had moved back in with my mum and dad because I couldn't cope with being alone. I know I would have drunk myself to death if I had stayed living on my own. The last year before coming here to New Life I realized that I had to be in a place where I could be looked after and that's what my mum did.

At SADAS they said "What are your strategies for not drinking at the airport?" and everything like that and that was a really good idea, to prepare myself for tempting situations that I would inevitably face once I was out in the big wide world on my own.

I thought I would come to New Life as a volunteer but within days of arriving I realized that I needed to be a resident and work on my issues. Despite all the counseling I have still got loads of unresolved stuff bubbling away just under the surface. The program itself is incredible. It's really challenging but the inter-esting part of it is that every time I feel something arise in me there will be a workshop that deals with that very issue or someone will hand me a book that answers my questions. It'll be presented to me, like with my current issue of expressing my feelings, it has just come up in the workshop on feelings this week.

I had a session with one of my life coaches here the other day and she said "How are you?" and I said "Fine" so she said "What's going on with your feet?" because I was tapping my feet so she said "Close your eyes, go inside, get in touch with the deeper feeling by breathing, bypass the mind, go into the feeling" and what came up was amazing. At the end of the session I felt a flow of unconditional love. All the time I was thinking I needed drink and drugs to make me feel better about myself but that feeling I was seeking is actually inside me, that euphoria, that peace, it's there. I don't need drugs. I can tap into that and it's more powerful than any drug.

I actually went to my first AA meeting ever yesterday. It was Dirty who suggested that I go. He said New Year's Eve is the most important day to go because everyone gets drunk on that day. So I went and it's difficult, you know, when it's your turn to speak and everyone's like "Hi, I'm John and I'm an alcoholic" and I'd never said that before. I told them that when it was my turn to speak, I wasn't comfortable with using that term. I was fiddling with a bit of paper and folding it up. I couldn't look up when I spoke. I didn't make eye contact with anybody. I just said "My name is Liam and I'm an alcoholic and the way that I define it is that when I drink I can't stop."

I think it was quite brave of me to go into the AA meeting, labeling myself as an alcoholic even though I am. Is it possible to be a 'bit' alcoholic? But I guess you either are or you aren't and I am. It's hard for me to admit that but it's the truth. I might do the 12 steps sometime in the future but not yet.

Right now I'm still learning about how mindfulness can help me with my longstanding issues around alcohol, drugs, self-worth and depression. To me, mindfulness simply means 'present moment awareness', not allowing myself to be distracted by what's happening around me. When I practice being in the moment I notice that my thoughts are clearer, more distinct. If you compare it to the sky, then normally my mind is dark and overcast with loads of clouds. When I meditate, any thought that arises is like a single cloud in the sky. From that clarity of mind I am able to act with more clarity. I take action for self, then actions for the others around me and then the wider world. Community living is a great testing ground because it is full of inherent challenges. I'm trying to lose my ego-self which is helping me to find my place in the community.

I've noticed that when I practice mindfulness I appreciate things more, like the beauty of nature around me. I always find walking in solitude gives me clarity especially in hard times. The walking meditations around the lakes have been truly mindful – always the same but always different, always different and always more beautiful. I realize I have missed so much because I have not really been present for most of my life.

When I become the observer I witness what is happening from the inside out. Clarity is created via openness to the source. When I place my consciousness on a single subject, object or view I can see with precision. When I am in that clear, still space it's like I can step back and recognize all my addictions. I can see my addictive behavior more clearly than I ever have done, as if I am viewing it on a TV screen, brought front and center to my attention to be acknowledged. It is part of me and not distinct from me. I'm learning to accept that fact.

A couple of phrases that I have found helpful as I go through my healing process are: 'Wherever You Go There You Are' and 'Be Here Now'.

But for me the key to my recovery from all addictions, maladies and challenges is 'Tonglen on the spot'. Tonglen simply means to completely accept everything that is happening. As Chögyam Trungpa Rinpoche puts it:

> The everyday practice is simply to develop a complete acceptance and openness to all situations and emotions, and to all people, experiencing everything totally without mental reservations and blockages, so that one never withdraws or centralizes onto oneself.

It's letting go of that resistance. Instead of blocking the flow of life I am learning to open up to it. It's a great feeling!

Before coming to New Life I used to think that meditation was sitting cross-legged on the floor with your eyes closed but now I understand that you can be in meditation all the time, like when you're walking down the street or eating your lunch or washing up. So meditation is mindfulness, just being fully present in the moment. Eckhart Tolle's book *The Power of Now* has been a great help to me as I'm shifting from my old way of being into my 'Tonglen' way of being.

All the connections I have made here have been incredible. In this community nobody feels they have to be something they are not. The challenge is to drop the mask that we normally show the world but you need confidence to do it and here it's a safe place to do that and once you've done it for the first time it just gets easier.

Regarding alcoholism, I would say that it's best to make the commitment to stop drinking altogether rather than just cutting down or trying to keep it under control. You can't control it if you have an alcohol addiction problem. Alcohol had power over me. I realize that. I haven't touched anything for 100 days, the longest I have ever done. I have reached this point and it's a watershed moment. I can't be complacent about it though. Complacency is my biggest obstacle, my biggest enemy. I need to stop myself going out and having a drink to celebrate the fact that I haven't drunk for so long…

Alain's Story

I'm 34 years old and I'm from Tahiti. I say I'm from Tahiti because that's where I grew up but actually I was born in France. I'm the firstborn of three children and I am the only male child in the whole family. When I was 6 months old my family moved to Tahiti and that's where I stayed until the age of 18 which is when I left to further my studies. I had four majors so I studied biology, Japanese, veterinary science and then business, finance and management for the hospitality industry, specializing in five-star resorts for Tahiti. I didn't finish my veterinary degree but I qualified on the first part so I'm able to work in the vet pharmaceutical industry but I can't set up and practice as a vet because I missed 2 years of study.

My first experience of drugs was during my childhood. As a child I was medicated because I was considered to be 'borderline'. That's a fashionable term for a certain psychological state. It's the tendency to act impulsively and have outbursts of emotion. I'm very, very emotive… emotional… I always was, even as a child, and my mum was very worried about me being too emotional or not being happy enough. I think she was afraid of me becoming depressed so at a very young age, like 5 years old, I was sent to see a child psychiatrist and consequently I was prescribed medication. You could say that that was the beginning of my addiction issues. Five is a very young age to be taking drugs!

The thing is that not only were my parents psychologists but my mother was actually involved in addiction counseling. My dad is a rehabilitation doctor with multiple degrees. He just works and makes money. He's very good at his work but because he's such a workaholic he's always been an absent father. He was never there for me when I was growing up because he was always out at work. My mum did most of the parenting. So as I said, I was on medication pretty young and that just about sums up the relationship I had with my mum: money and medication. She just has always provided me with those two things and not much else. Because of her work she had legal access to prescription medication so I guess you could say that she was my main drug provider. That's not the usual way it goes! I managed to break the pattern not long ago but up until quite recently she continued to send me big packages of medication even when I was traveling or living abroad. There was always something for me to take, always a selection of various mood-altering tablets, so I just took them. I took them because they were there. I was just like a pill child, just popping pills all the time, even if there was no particular reason to do so.

We didn't have much love or affection at home. I remember my mother having frequent random fits of violence and then she would go back to normal. My dad wasn't like that, just my mother. She's a very emotional person too. She would just get mad for a few seconds and then be really sorry afterwards. She just hit me with anything that was around. She hit me with a stick, her hand... Once I accidentally made a dent in my saxophone and when she saw it she just went absolutely crazy and hit me in the face with it. Then the next second when she realized what she had done she went back to just being scolding. She would just go really mad when I did bad things so I was kind of afraid of her. In fact everybody in the family was afraid of her.

She was like a bomb that could go off at any time. I don't know if you can imagine what it was like to live in such a state of constant high alert. It was stressful but I didn't know any other way of living.

I found it impossible to be truthful to her about my feelings because I didn't want to upset her. If I ever said I felt bad then she would 'blackmail' me by saying "Oh, why are you feeling bad? When you feel bad you make me feel bad" so basically I'm always fine, I always say that I'm fine. It's not true but it's what she wants to hear. I would say that I'm always paranoid and on the lookout for anything. Anything hiding…

I was always trying not to upset her in any way. We're very, very close. That's where the borderline thing comes in. We fused basically, I was just always very close with her but yet I was always resenting it. Everything I did was based upon what she wanted or what I thought she wanted. I even started dieting with her at the age of 12 or 13, just sharing every single part of her life with her and so I still have an eating disorder now.

Mum was 23 years old when she had me. Her mother had a really bad experience at the age of 17 and it really changed her. She fled under the German bombs from the Luxembourg border and consequently she suffered from shell shock and post-traumatic stress. Later on in life, when she had her family, she would take it out on her kids, her stress. So my mum suffered from her own mother's crazy behavior. In fact, when she got old I remember my grandmother would suddenly jump as if she was trying to avoid the bombs and she would go and hide under the table, reliving that wartime experience over and over again. My grandmother had literally fled as the bombs were falling from the sky all around her. I can hardly imagine what that experience must have been like for a 17-year-old and in those days post-traumatic stress disorder was not yet widely recognized so she received no psychological help. She simply carried the trauma within her until the day that she died.

Growing up in Tahiti I never felt very safe, certainly not at school. Kids can be very mean towards each other and there was a lot of racism so I often got into fights. I was a good fighter because I never backed off. I didn't know how to stop a fight. I had these fits of rage and would just get out of control, and keep on punching and kicking. I made friends by fighting. That's how people made friends at my school. I would fight a guy and the next day he would be my friend. I earned respect because of my ability to fight and never back off. It helped that by the age of 15 I was already the size I am now so everybody stopped picking on me because I was unbeatable. I have broad shoulders and a very powerful physique because I used to do gymnastics at international level.

After finishing high school I stayed in Tahiti in order to get my driving license and then at the age of 18 I went to France. I had started university in Tahiti but I needed to leave to continue my education. Besides that, I just couldn't take the island anymore. I needed to break free from my home life. I was feeling stifled, suffocated. I was fed up with the same streets, the same people, the same things. Nothing changes there. So I decided to go to Strasbourg because some of my extended family was living there. I knew that it was time to move on.

After I left Tahiti I was kind of depressed, using whatever drugs and alcohol I could find to cope with life. I wasn't being active anymore. I stopped doing gymnastics and I just became more and more depressed, constantly popping pills and eating and everything. I was getting fat because I was eating too much and what with the side effects of the medication I just put on lots of weight. The medication makes me eat a lot. Looking back I think that the shock of coming out of Tahiti and meeting the real world was too much of an adjustment for me. Everything was totally different in mainland Europe. I was spending a lot of time alone. My weight shot up to 130kg and then I failed an exam for the first time ever. It was the second session of veterinary studies and I freaked out over it. I thought 'For fuck's sake' so then I did a diet for 2 and a half months and lost 45kg. That was the first time I did a really harsh diet. I stopped eating carbohydrates for a year. Maybe it was a control thing. I couldn't control everything in my life but I could control my weight through not eating.

Then I began to look for the hardest things I could do so I started to learn how to touch-type because I can't stand typing. I got really good at it so then I set myself another challenge, to learn one of the hardest languages in the world which is Japanese. I didn't really give a fuck about Japan. In fact I don't really like Japan. I started studying the Japanese language and I studied really hard and at the same time that I started learning the language I also started studying biology. After a while I thought 'This is too slow, I need to go fast track' so I said to my teachers "You guys are too slow so what can I do to speed things up?" They said I could apply to go to Japan for a scholarship but there was only 3 days before the closing date. I told my teachers I didn't like what they were teaching and I said "I want to fuck off so give me a reference letter so that I can get away." They wanted me to become a biology teacher in a high school but I said "No fucking way, I'm leaving." I got the scholarship in Japan and also got my first girlfriend there, a German girl.

So I learned Japanese. I didn't put much effort into it but I find languages easy so soon I could speak it okay and I got my degree in Japanese. When I wasn't studying I spent my time spending money and doing a bit of traveling, including spending 2 months in Thailand. I didn't like Japan so I decided I was going to come and live in Thailand to study the Thai languages and international relations. I had thought about going to Paris. I had the idea to become a diplomat or whatever, then my parents said "Well, you always wanted to become a vet so why don't you do veterinary studies?" That wasn't really true but it just so happened that a friend of mine from Tahiti was studying to be a vet in Belgium so I decided I might as well do it and I thought

'That's it' and I went to Belgium. When I got there I just didn't study at all. I started getting into a real lot of drugs because as a veterinary student I had access to drugs like ketamine. Also, Belgium is a major point in Europe for drug dealers so I had access to a lot of stuff, but not in such large amounts that I really got into trouble with it. At that time I was more into speed and amphetamines. I mean cocaine wasn't even my thing. That came later. I would smoke it or do free basing, and sniffing. I didn't really like it that much. Speed and crystal meth is much better and it's very cheap in Belgium. Usually I mix my drugs. I don't take just one drug at a time. Anyway, whatever illegal drugs I was taking were always being taken alongside the legal prescription drugs from my mother.

The time in Belgium wasn't my first encounter with drugs as I had got quite heavily into amphetamines in Japan. They're a kind of uppers. It's what you give ADHD people to keep them focused and they were easy to get hold of.

I got the drugs from friends, along with pot and alcohol. I mean I was already definitely an alcoholic but a social one. I didn't tend to drink alone in those days. That would come later on. I smoked a lot of pot. In fact I smoked anything I could get hold of. I wasn't fussy, I wasn't picky. I just took whatever was available because it's a limited market out there in Japan. Quite different to Tahiti where cannabis grows everywhere so it's really easy to get hold of. On Tahiti, first you learn to smoke pot and then cigarettes, it's that way round. I was smoking cannabis regularly by the age of 12. That was also the age I started drinking for the first time, the first time I got completely drunk. My first drink was whiskey, vodka and gin mixed up without water. Also pastis. It's French alcohol, 50% proof, turns white when you add water but I used to drink it neat. So I carried on drinking and smoking pot from the age of 12 and at the same time I was still taking prescription drugs. I think that's what got me into the other drugs because it really facilitates the addiction, especially with alcohol. I don't think you can get addicted to pot, not physically, but you can have a psychological addiction. In fact you can have a psychological addiction to anything.

It took me a long time to realize that I had an addiction problem. The reason I didn't realize sooner was because I could go for really long periods without using the illegals and then I would crash. But all the time I was taking the so-called legal drugs, like the sleeping tablets and mood stabilizers and they're powerful. I was constantly popping pills, that's the thing. I had the prescription drugs, only I don't get them prescribed, I just got huge packs of them sent to me by my mum. I'm talking about really strong stuff but I was using them like homoeopathic drugs. I didn't know how strong they were until I went to the doctor in Belgium and told him what I was taking and how much of it and he said "Are you fucking crazy?" I was taking benzos mostly and hypnotics and sleeping pills, very strong – the ones you use for jet lag. I have been using them to sleep since I was a kid. I quit those for the first time in my life when I got here to New Life. That's when I stopped everything, even my medication like the mood stabilizer because I couldn't be bothered to carry on getting my liver tested every 2 weeks to see if I was being poisoned. The mood stabilizer drug is just like lithium, it's very strong. It's called Tegretol but when you're taking it you have to have your blood tested regularly because it's so bloody toxic. You have to watch the dosage on that one particularly carefully, more so than any of the others I was taking. Tegretol and lithium work in a similar way, robbing you of the highs and lows. It deadens you, kind of robs you of your personality because you don't like the same things that you liked before, things like music and such like. A lot of stuff you don't appreciate anymore.

I came to New Life more than a year ago and when I got here I stopped all my medication, all drugs and all alcohol. I remained clean until one month ago when I fucked up on alcohol and pot.

The thing is I had stopped my medication so I ended up being overactive. I went into a hyper state. They say I have bipolar but I don't believe in that because I think borderline is kind of the same thing. You just do stuff, become really active and gradually you do more and more and you eat less and less and sleep less and at some point you just stop sleeping and stop eating. You're on a high. It's a manic state – you just enjoy yourself and you don't feel the need to rest or eat anymore. I'm not joking when I say that I probably slept no more than 1 or 2 hours a night during those 3 weeks. I knew I was going to go down at some point. That's the thing with a high. What goes up must come down. I could see where I was heading because you just have to crash and I could see the crash coming. I usually last longer in the manic state than I did this time because I'm usually still taking drugs but of course here at New Life I wasn't taking drugs, not even the legal ones. That was my choice. We're obviously allowed to take legal drugs and medication here. I told the staff I couldn't sleep. I tried lots of things because I didn't want to go back on medication drugs. That would remind me of the mental hospitals and I just don't ever want to go back there. I was in there five times when I lived in Paris. I crash and when that happens I just binge and I'm just in such a confused state that it takes me several weeks to come back out of it. I go crazy. I become paranoid and I have hallucinations. I see stuff moving, I stop being able to sleep and I see dark shapes all around, dark shadowy shapes, there's always something moving. I can't look at them directly as they shape shift. Then when I close my eyes I get flashes and if I look at the walls I can see a movie, just a movie like at the cinema. And sometimes when I close my eyes I get assaulted by a lot of gore and flesh, really weird stuff. Like blood and guts, the sort of images you might see in a horror film.

When I came down I ended up in hospital. I didn't try and kill myself this time, I just cut myself so now I have a few more scars and then I stopped which is a kind of improvement. Usually when I'm coming down I really cut myself hard. The last three times it happened – in Paris – I ended up in the hospital. The same thing happened twice in Tahiti where I got sectioned for 2 months.

When I came out of it this time I said that I would not go through the same kind of confusion again. I got very, very high and I decided that when I came down and it all started going crazy that I would just cut a little bit, just enough to control it. So this time when I saw and felt the crash coming I went out and got myself a hotel room and got smashed out of my head on alcohol. I drank so much. At first that helped but I had to cut to get out of it when alcohol wasn't helping anymore. I just get into anxiety, fits of panic, so high. If I cut myself it keeps me focused. It's a release.

I felt so guilty like why would I even do that but I'm such a different person when I'm in that state. I just don't give a shit anymore. Usually I'm just so nice but when I get high I'm totally uninhibited and I do stuff like I just couldn't believe I could do, things like being really mean. I really hurt people. I just know what I want somehow when I'm out of my head and there's nothing stopping me, nothing saying I shouldn't do that and I like that feeling of course because it's a release. That's why I try and lock myself up when I get those feelings because I'm aware that I don't have control and that I might do stupid things. So after I cut myself and saw the blood spurting everywhere – all over the hotel room – I called David and said "Get me out of here" and he came to the hotel to get me and brought me back here. (David is a staff member at New Life.)

There are consequences for using illegal drugs and/or alcohol at New Life, namely a 15-day suspension so I have to leave for 15 days and that is why I'm going to the monastery. I have spent time in monasteries before. I used to be a monk and I even spent a month as a wandering monk. Actually I became a monk just for that purpose. I have always wanted to experience what it would be like to live in that way because I believe it is the authentic, original practice the Buddha taught. I learned a lot during those days spent wandering. I learned to observe my mind as I wandered and it almost drove me crazy. It is a very hard practice that makes no sense to the Western mind. There's no doubt about it, it's an extreme practice. In a way it's like a very long walking meditation. As I wandered I tried to recite mantras in my mind 24/7 but it was hard and I actually lost 24 kilos in less than 4 weeks through lack of food, stress, difficult living conditions and constant walking. Although it was a difficult experience it was very interesting and I will probably do it again at some point in the future.

When I returned from my wandering I stayed as a monk in the monastery at Thamkrabok to work in the detox center. I spent time helping the addicts. It's the detox monastery. I was there for 5 and a half months. I just wanted to be a monk, something I wanted 15 years ago, so I figured if I came here to New Life to deal with my issues and addictions first then I could go off and become a monk. Life as a monk was too easy for me and I felt afraid to come back to New Life. I chose the option that I feared. That's what I do.

The most useful thing I have learned at New Life is to open up without fear. I have also learned a lot about meditation and mindfulness. People project so much around the term 'mindfulness' but really, all it is about is being in the here and now. Just experience the moment without trying to analyze or judge it. It's a very simple thing yet it's very hard to put into practice. I would say that it's especially hard to implement with people who have just come out of drug addiction, alcoholism or depression but it is the only way. It's very painful but it works, just sitting with the craving until it passes, not judging the craving, just feeling it, allowing it to arise but not attaching to it. The craving passes. Really, it does! Cravings come and go. I guess the main difficulty is being able to give someone the faith that anything goes away, even the craving. That can't be taught. It has to be experienced.

I am aware that I usually choose the hard path for myself. I might become a monk again one day. I'm wondering whether I might be one in the next few weeks. Maybe I will make this decision soon. I'm 34 now. It's my birthday today. Maybe it's time...

Kate's Story

I found New Life as a result of a bad breakup with an active alcoholic. He had been transferred to the Maldives for work and I was scheduled to go down and visit him when he publicly humiliated me on Facebook. That incident was just indicative of the abuse that had been going on for the last 6 months of our relationship so I was in a very small space, feeling very confused and hurt and I was in need of healing. I did a Google search for a yoga retreat in Thailand because that's where I live and that's when I found New Life. I immediately felt myself being drawn here. It was almost physical, the draw was so strong. I could even say it was magnetic! I booked a week here, the week I would have been in the Maldives with him if we hadn't split up.

While I was recovering in this safe and supportive space, he was in the Maldives on a week-long bender. I heard that he was hospitalized after 7 days of solid drinking and after that he was sent to Thamkrabok to detox. I didn't know that there was a connection between Thamkrabok monastery and New Life. People often come to New Life after their vomiting detox so it was quite a shock to me when I discovered that the founders of New Life had both been at Thamkrabok.

So, while Ruben was going through his vomiting detox at Thamkrabok, I was going through some very powerful healing experiences here that allowed me to let go of a lot of pain and trauma that I had carried throughout that relationship. I stayed at New Life for 2 weeks immediately after the breakup and I returned home feeling much stronger. Before I left I booked in advance for the Christmas holidays, knowing that by that time my ex would be out of the monastery and probably back in Bangkok – which he is. He's there now. Bangkok is the city where we live and where we met. He showed up the week before Christmas so I was very pleased that I had planned ahead so that I had somewhere to go. I came here to receive the help that I needed to cope with the second step of this difficult experience of my relationship breakdown.

I was feeling so alone after the breakup. I didn't know where to go, who to turn to, how to cope. Now I'm feeling a bit stronger and more clear-headed. I know that I need to remove certain people from my life. I'm talking about Ruben and the circles he moves in. It is time to just move on to the next chapter of my life, whatever that is.

Every morning here at New Life I have been attending the early morning yoga. One morning my body began to shake and shake. I was taken aback and a little bit afraid at first. What I didn't realize was that I was actually having a tremor release experience. It had happened involuntarily. My entire body began to shake and convulse. It was as if something in my brain knew that this is what I needed and so I let it happen. I lay down and grabbed my knees to my chest and didn't try and control the shaking. People pay money for this sort of thing. I'm so smart I have done it for myself! It felt really healing, like a massive shift of energy.

My life has had many chapters. The current one is here in Thailand where I now live. How did I find my way to Thailand? Well, at the end of 2008 the economy in the USA was not good so I thought I would come out to Asia for 3 weeks and then return home but I ended up staying in Asia for 6 months. I traveled around, visiting many beautiful places but wherever I traveled to I always found myself being drawn back to Bangkok. For some reason I always felt at home in that city.

After a wonderful few months exploring Thailand I returned to New York but it was hard being back there. The cold, the tiredness and the depression hit me hard. I began to think about returning to Bangkok. I had the feeling that if I didn't go I would always regret it so I made the courageous decision to follow my heart and leave my apartment in New York. I packed up my stuff, shut the door behind me and moved out here. I knew I would be able to cope financially by teaching English. I fell into that very easily and I have been able to survive quite well.

Living in Thailand is a world away from my old life. I was born in a small town in upstate New York. I come from a large family. I have six sisters and one brother. One of my sisters is my twin. We were full term and my mum didn't know she was having twins until we were born. My sister popped out and then I appeared. Everybody was very shocked by my unscheduled arrival! We were both very tiny when we were born. I was 3lb 11 ounces so I was put straight into an incubator at birth and stayed there for a month. I didn't get reunited with my mum until I was 4 weeks old. Mum wasn't able to hold me at all during my first weeks on earth, only the nurses could handle me. For that first month I was even disconnected from my twin. Maybe that's where my fierce independent streak comes from.

So I grew up in this big family with everything that comes along with living in a big family. Mum used to really lose it with us. My sister and I think she might have a borderline personality disorder. She's a rage-aholic, using her children as pawns against each other. She was constantly verbally abusive to my father and sometimes even physically abusive towards him. He is a recovering alcoholic. Apparently he stopped drinking after the birth of the first four of his kids.

I never knew him to drink. I had no idea about his past until the day of his funeral. All these people turned up to say their last goodbyes and when I asked who they were I was told they were 'Daddy's friends'. It turned out they were all from his AA group.

That's when I discovered that my dad had been an alcoholic. My dad's father was an alcoholic too and so is one of my brothers and two of my sisters. As you can see, it's in the family!

My mum and dad are both Greek by descent and I had a Greek Orthodox Church upbringing. My father owned a popular restaurant and we lived in the apartment above it. It was quite a crowded home. Me and my twin slept in my parents' bedroom until the age of 4. I have a really good memory that goes back a long way. I can even remember being in my pram.

I left home at the age of 18. I had watched my brother and my sisters going away to college and returning to work in the family restaurant but I didn't want to do that. When I was 12 years old I wrote in my diary, 'I will never live in this town when I grow up.' I kept that vow.

I went to college in Manhattan and studied art. It was always clear that I had a natural talent for design. It's a talent I was born with. I guess it could be called a gift. After graduation I soon found work, working on international magazines and in world-famous publishing houses. I was quite ambitious because I was out to prove myself. You see, my brother was the prince of the world as he was the only boy in the family. The rest of us were 'just girls'. My reaction to that injustice was that I was going to show them, I would be successful to prove that I wasn't 'just' a girl. And I was successful. I became a graphic designer on one of the top fashion magazines.

After my dad died I moved to Washington on my own. In fact I have spent most of my life living alone. I had a conversation with my dad after he died and he said he could be with me at any time. I'm a natural psychic but I have never developed my gift to its full potential.

Once, when I went to the Grand Canyon I could feel the presence of my dad in the car. It was a really strong feeling. I was there at sunset and it really felt as if he was standing right there beside me, so much so that I was actually moved to tears. When

I showed my mum the pictures of the sunset I had taken she said "Oh the Grand Canyon, that's one place that your dad always wanted to visit."

After Washington I ended up moving to the west coast and got an amazing job with a good wage. I have won national awards and acclaim for my work. I feel really blessed that I have been given the gift of design because my talent has opened so many doors for me.

When I came to Bangkok it was a huge life change. I came alone but I already knew a couple of people here who I had met on my TEFL course. I had no apartment to go to but I soon found one and then I met Ruben in a club. He's Swiss and he is an alcoholic. He hid it quite well at first but after the first month he began to get very drunk when we were together. The first time it happened he said he was really sorry and it wouldn't happen again. Maybe I'm naive... or stupid. I grew up in an alcoholic family so I ought to have known because of course it did happen again... and again... and again. It happened more and more frequently and he would even wake up in the morning with the DTs and have to go and have a shot. I don't know why I stayed with him. I guess part of me wanted to help him and partly because he did offer me a sense of community that I didn't have as he had an established group of friends like a 'gang' that I could belong to. That gave me a sense of belonging. My loneliness wanted that so I made a lot of concessions. We could do things together, not just drinking but go out to the coast for a weekend.

The abuse within the relationship started small, just little put-downs and remarks but gradually it got worse. Towards the end it was really, really horrible. I no longer knew who I was. People who have known me for years told me that I had changed, that I was no longer the person they used to know. I wasn't that person who had won all those awards and held down prestigious jobs. I used to say to myself, 'Why are you letting this person treat you like this?' It's still a mystery to me why I allowed him to treat me so badly. Why did I not just walk away? I was so angry at myself and angry at him.

I do believe that things happen for a reason even though we can't usually see the reason at the time. At least I'm aware enough to be able to step back and look at myself. It's not my pattern to be with someone like that but I know that we do draw to ourselves what is familiar and the world of alcohol is a familiar world for me. You see, I'm no angel myself. I have used alcohol as a crutch many times in my past. Before I left New York I was drinking an awful lot. I had enough self-awareness to recognize that my alcohol consumption was out of control and so I sent myself to AA for 6 months. I needed to figure out why I was drinking. It was okay at the beginning but towards the end of that time I hated the weekly AA meeting and wanted to stop going but I needed to go to touch base in the group once a week for the support that it gave me. But then I found out about Smart Recovery. It was started by a man named Albert Ellis who has passed away now but the Institute is still in operation in Park Avenue. They use motivational, behavioral and cognitive methods to help people recover from addictive behavior. They also run a network of self-help meetings and also partner with care professionals.

I was so happy to have found Smart Recovery because I much prefer their approach to the approach of AA. They deal with it from the core which just suits me better. When you go along to AA the first thing you have to do is to admit that you are an alcoholic. You literally say, "My name is X and I am an alcoholic." Smart Recovery takes a completely different approach. They don't think labels help with recovery and so they are avoided. People are not called 'addicts' or 'alcoholics' or anything. They also have an online community so that I can touch base from anywhere in the world. That's really helpful.

At Smart Recovery they suggest we ask ourselves why we are

acting in the way we are, like asking ourselves why we are making certain choices. They say that nobody shoved that bottle into your hand and forced the alcohol down your throat. Nobody stuck that syringe of heroin into your body. So why make those choices, choices that do not serve you?

I gained a lot from attending that group, meeting up with other people who were in the process of dealing with their issues.

My drinking in Thailand hasn't been too bad. It got a little bad when I started getting a bit pissed on the weekends but when I met Ruben my drinking really escalated. It was bound to. Hanging out with an alcoholic? I went right back to where I was when I had sent myself to AA. Why was I choosing to drink so much? Why was I making that choice? It wasn't a good choice. All that drinking doesn't help with my depression and low self-esteem. You know that alcohol is a depressant.

So I've had quite a few issues to look at during my time here at New Life. It has been very helpful and I can see now that it's thanks to that abusive relationship that I found New Life so at least something good has come out of it!

A few months ago I could never have foreseen that I would feel like that because I was so angry at him, so angry with myself, just depressed and horrible. Although that was a difficult time and I experienced some challenging emotions, I now find that when I practice mindfulness my emotions balance themselves. I am able to stop my mental chatter when I focus on my breath and that's a wonderful thing to be able to do. I feel peace when I concentrate on letting go.

Amber's Story

I was born in Glasgow in Scotland, 6 weeks early, feet first and with severe jaundice. I was rushed straight to intensive care for treatment so Mum didn't see me for those first few hours. Despite that and the fact that I was never breastfed I still had a very close bond with my mum.

My mum was quite young when she had me. Mum and Dad had met in their teens and had been together for 6 years by the time I was born. I was their second child. I have an older sister. While she was pregnant with me, Mum discovered that my dad was having an affair. They tried to make the marriage work but Mum and Dad finally split up when I was 3 months old. When Dad left her, my mum was left alone with me – a newborn baby – and a 5-year-old. My sister helped to look after me so the three of us became very bonded.

I don't have many early memories but I know that me, Mum and my sister moved to a council house in Manchester when I was 3 years old. It was a long way from my dad but I didn't mind because I didn't really have much of a bond with him. My sister did have a bond and she was upset because we were living so far away. I sometimes went to visit him and my stepmum but I never felt close to them. I think he kind of saw me as his guilt.

When I was 5 my mum met my stepdad and married him. I was close to him from day one but my sister didn't like him. He was a psychiatric nurse. Shortly after his arrival on the scene the family started to split. It was me, Mum and Perry together and my sister separate. He was very clever and manipulated the situation. My sister got very sulky and she started taking drugs at an early age. I was labeled as the good daughter and she was referred to as the bad one. There were lots of arguments in the house and things weren't all good.

I went through puberty early and in the bathroom we had quite a big keyhole. One day I was getting undressed and for some reason I looked through the keyhole and saw my stepdad's eye. I went downstairs and said "Perry's a pervert" but my mum didn't really take any notice. Also, my sister used to call him 'The P'. P stood for pervert. I remember my sister saying things like "I'm going to sunbathe but don't let Perry see me." We never ever talked about our experiences with Perry. He would perv with my friends too but I blocked it all.

During the ages 9 to 15 his perving got worse. He would inappropriately touch me but again I would block it because I had a good relationship with him and I didn't want to spoil it. But I always felt uneasy in the bathroom and I used to cover up the keyhole. This went on for a long time, this sense of unease in the house and anytime I was around Perry.

Then when I was 9 my sister tried to commit suicide. She had overdosed on her epilepsy tablets, washing them down with alcohol. She was only 14 years old. I heard her in the middle of the night and I found her passed out in her bedroom. Perry saved her. While she was in the hospital she wanted to tell the doctors about the sexual abuse that she was being subjected to by Perry but my real dad had said that if he ever found out that anything was going on, he would kill Perry. My sister didn't want her dad going to prison for murder so she didn't say anything.

That night when she was in hospital my stepdad got into bed with me and said he wanted to pray with me because he was very religious but it felt wrong. I didn't want him in my bed. He was always doing things I didn't like, for example dropping his towel 'accidentally' after having a shower, just really weird things that he shouldn't have been doing.

My mum was seemingly unaware. I shouted "Perry is a pervert!" on various occasions but I don't know if she even heard me. I remember kicking the fridge and things like that in my... what... anger? Frustration? Distress?

So my stepdad had created this split in the family and had pushed my sister away from us all but when my sister got pregnant I got close to her again. I was really excited about the baby and we bonded over that. She was only 16 but she kept the baby.

My mum and Perry were trying for a baby but couldn't get pregnant so at that point my stepdad kicked my sister out because he didn't want her to have the baby in their house. She went to live with my dad. He was still with the woman that he had the affair with and had another daughter with her. He never had a son although he would have liked one.

My sister had the baby but 3 months later she argued with my dad and she returned to Manchester to live in a council place. I was very involved with her son Jo, looking after him and taking him out.

Then when I was 13 my mum went to America for a holiday and she fell in love with a guy she met there. She didn't want this to happen but in the end she had to accept it. When we came back to London my mum moved into the spare room. She couldn't make her marriage work so in the end she left Perry. He got to keep the council house and Mum and I moved to a flat 10 minutes away. I was devastated to leave the house, my room, the cats and the garden. After all, this had been my home since the age of 3.

I still used to go and see Perry because I had a good relationship with him. He was my dad really.

After meeting this new man my mum started going off to America for several months at a time to visit him and she would leave me alone with Perry. I was only 14 and I was still at school so I couldn't go with her. I remember hearing my sister say to my mum, "Watch Perry with Amber, he's always tickling her and touching her." I think she suspected something wasn't right and it was true. It was uncomfortable. I had a boyfriend by that age but that didn't stop Perry the perv. I was starting to be unable to block what he was doing and I would say "Get off me, don't touch me." One night he took me to the cinema and he was treating me like his girlfriend and then he tried it on in the cinema and I physically pushed him away and said no. That was the first time I had pushed him away like that.

He wanted to get back with my mum and he kept me up all night one night. He was having these visions because he used to have these holy visions and he drew pictures of them and things and after one of these visions he was convinced he was going to get back with my mum. That was the first time I remember thinking, 'Crikey, you're a bit crazy!' He was this really crazy guy yet he was in a well-respected position working as a nurse in a major hospital.

I was so glad when my mum got back. The day after she came home my sister came over to visit and I said "Thank God you're back because I don't like being left alone with Perry. He's a pervert." My sister said "I don't believe it! Has he been doing it to you too?" So we went and told Mum and she took us over to his house and he admitted it. I never saw him again, not until I was 18.

Then, when I was 18 I wanted some answers to what had happened. My mum didn't see him anymore but she let me go because I wanted to go and see him and to try and make sense of it all. I went out with him for the day but he was still acting strange.

Mum was a bit 'head in the sand'. After his perving came out in the open Mum said that Perry had once cried and said he had touched his patient's breasts but she hadn't told anyone or done anything about it.

So Perry was out of my life and now my mum had a boyfriend. I didn't accept Steve for ages. I didn't want to be friends with him but when I saw how happy my mum was I eventually accepted the situation.

At 17 my sister was date raped and contracted HIV. Someone had spiked her drink and raped her. That was devastating to me. It was not long after this that I started smoking and drinking. I was getting into boys and I lost my virginity at 14. Acid was my first drug at 14, then speed at 15. I was smoking dope and drinking spirits. I started going to raves at the age of 15 and got into the rave scene big time. I was still at school so I would make money by selling speed at the club. I went to squat and warehouse parties. They were massive gatherings. It was amazing, great fun. I was a real party animal. I could go three nights in a row, out dancing all night and getting out of my head.

You could get into some places for free and there was a sheet of acid that you could just tear a bit off if you wanted a trip.

At the age of 17 I moved in with a group of friends just down the road from my mum's place. In this house I got into ketamine which is used as a horse tranquilizer but it's also used as an anesthetic for children. It's not an opiate or anything, it's an anesthetic. We were into it big time. For 6 months straight I was doing it every single day. I was working in a factory at that time which was really monotonous work. What I really wanted to do was art and so I applied and got a place at college. That's when my mum moved away to Ireland with Steve but she kept the flat on in London for my sake.

When I was 18 I met Greg, a real hippy guy, and he introduced me to the festival world and we used to experiment with drugs. I finished my degree and then got into the British festival scene. We set up this hemp café, selling hemp burgers and things, doing the smaller hippy festivals. I was really happy in my life at this time. However, there was always ketamine around and I realized I'd gone a bit too far with it. I was smoking pot every day and Greg was dealing hash and skunk. It comes as a liquid and you heat it to turn it into a powder, then you snort it. I broke up with Greg after 2 years because I felt smothered by him.

After my degree I got work in a graphic design studio and I loved it. I worked there for 6 to 7 years. I was going to parties at weekends and I was getting drunk. I'd always go too far with alcohol and I'd be the one that had to be carried home. I only did that at weekends and maybe once or twice in the week. I was drinking wine, not spirits, but lots of it, enough to pass out so you can imagine how much I was drinking but I was managing to hold down this job.

When I was 25 I decided I wanted to travel and then I met Zak. He was from South Africa. I met him at a party the first time and then I bumped into him a few months later at a dealer's house. He was into cocaine so from day one we were taking loads of cocaine together. I was living with my sister at that point but soon we got a place with another couple and we started on crack. We'd spend all our money on it. Zak was dishonest with money from day one. He had been in prison and he'd had a rough life. It was all he knew. He'd rob anyone if he needed money. So there I was going to work each day and doing crack in the evenings and weekends and then I'd have to drink loads to come down off the crack or the ketamine.

We married when I was 27. Our plan was to go traveling so we saved up. For crack heads we were quite together. Well, that's not quite true. In reality it was me who was together because I saved all my money and he spent all his. We were living rent free at my sister's house which helped me to be able to save.

We had a Buddhist wedding in Thailand. It was a fantastic and wonderful wedding day. After our wedding we traveled to India and it was there that I tried heroin for the first time. Zak was an ex-addict and he'd been clean for 15 years but for some reason he decided he wanted to take some. We smoked it and I liked it the first time but the second time I tried it I didn't like it and didn't want to try it again. We did it a couple of times then it was forgotten about. We came back to England and moved in with my sister. Hers was a bit of a party house and at the time she was in a very volatile relationship. We were all taking drugs, not in front of them but behind our bedroom door so the kids couldn't see. She had a second child by now, a daughter, and I was quite a big part of the children's lives, helping to care for them, get them ready for school and so on. My sister had been dabbling with heroin for a while, smoking it now and again but she hadn't got hooked.

Me and Zak were doing loads of crack but I was still working, doing freelance and agency work and he was working as a welder. Then Zak bumped into an old friend from South Africa who was an addict he used to do heroin with. We spent the whole night with his friend doing drugs. His mate was doling out the crack and he said "Do you want to try heroin?" and he made me a syringe up and Zak did some, my sister did some, Zak's friend did some and so did I. He put the syringe in me and I passed out, slouched over. It was instant, I was out. I had gone blue and my sister was hysterical. Zak had to do mouth to mouth and that got me back. I woke up to my sister screaming and my reaction was "That was fucking wicked."

The next day my sister was still freaked out over what had happened and I vowed never to touch the stuff again. But I was hanging out with the same people as my sister and it was easy to get hold of heroin and my sister had started injecting it herself. And so we started doing it together, a kind of 'if you can't beat them join them' attitude. I soon became hooked. I would have a shot in the morning, go to work and have another shot when I got home.

I managed to get off it though. I went to the methadone clinic to ask for help but they were going to tell work about it so I said no to the methadone and got off by myself. It's easier the first time but it gets harder the longer you're on it.

I just kept getting hooked on heroin and then doing cold turkey to come off it. I did that a few times. I never got hooked for that long. I didn't want to be living the life of a junkie.

Then my sister lost her kids. Sara said she wanted to go and live with her dad and a few months later Jo said the same and we have never seen them since. Sara was 10 and Jo was 17 when they left. The boy Jo wasn't even his. It makes me want to be sick. I hate him. Losing the kids destroyed my sister. She felt too weak to fight and in a way she gave up. She was depressed and started taking more drugs, getting out of control with her addiction.

I had a lot to deal with at that time: the loss of the kids, the mistrust of Zak, the death of my cat and the suicide of my friend. She hung herself because her dad was abusing her and when she told the family they wouldn't believe her.

Zak was heavily into heroin and would always be leaving

needles around the house. I started to drink a lot and my sister was acting really shit. She was drunk and obnoxious and me and my mum couldn't cope with her. Then during one massive argument she screamed at us that Perry had made her have sex with her at the age of 13. We knew it was true so we went to the police the next day. In the police station I started telling them my story too and it got taken out of my hands completely. By this time he was head of department in the hospital. The year before this one of his patients had reported him for sexual abuse but she was too scared to take him to court. But with me they pressed charges against him and that's when my drinking got out of control. I would go and give my statements and then go home and get blind drunk. It got out of control in my head. The police were amazing but I wasn't having counseling to help me through. I think they offered it to me but if they did I didn't accept it. I can't remember. I just wanted to make the statements and then forget about it. I had good memories of my childhood because they were selective memories. When I was forced to confront the truth it was really upsetting. It was as if everything involving Perry was tainted. My childhood that had seemed okay felt spoiled, ruined. Every moment I had ever spent with him was forever tainted.

Because I was taking Perry to court, the girl who had originally backed down found the courage to charge him too. Then other patients started coming forward. He had admitted everything to his best friend who was a priest but he also said that he was going to deny it all in court. The priest told him that he had to admit the truth so it was good for us to have a vicar on our side. We had a strong case.

Perry was struggling while all of this was going on. He was sectioned and put on suicide watch. He was in the psychiatric hospital as a patient for over a year.

Then I split up with Zak. I was devastated. I just drank and cried, falling into a deep depression. My sister told my mum to come and get me and when we got to Mum's she told us that Perry had committed suicide by jumping off a cliff. I had every single emotion going on inside me, a whole jumble of chaotic and conflicting turmoil. I loved him but I hated him. I wanted him to pay for what he'd done but I didn't want him to hurt. I wanted him to own up but I wanted him to be okay. I wanted him to get the help he needed but I wanted the truth to be told. In a way I was quite relieved not to have to face my stepdad in court but I felt tremendous guilt, as if I was to blame for his suicide.

I was an out-and-out druggie by this time and my mum couldn't cope. She'd had enough of me and so had my sister. I was trying not to be a junkie. I had a heroin habit and that's why I had to drink. Heroin withdrawal is painful. When I can't get any my body aches and I can't sleep so the drinking lessens the pain. One week I was admitted to hospital 8 times in 7 days. I was lucky I didn't die with the amount of alcohol that was in my blood. While I was in hospital my mum found out I was using heroin because the doctors found the track marks on my arm. That was the first time she knew about my addiction.

My husband was HIV positive and we had shared needles and had unprotected sex once or twice so I took the test but luckily I didn't have it.

Then I met a guy called Rik and I ended up living with him in a shit hole. He hoards, doesn't use a bin and the house is full of needles. He has addiction problems big time. It was about this time that I stopped working. I just couldn't keep it up.

It was difficult living at Rik's so I went into a homeless hostel and went into detox. I was given some Subutex. It blocks heroin, literally stops it working, but they gave it to me in tablet form so I used to spit it out and carry on shooting up. My husband and I were back together but just as friends and by now I was getting my drugs from both Rik and Zak.

Most of my friends had given up on me by now. They had tried to help and failed. They couldn't cope with me and my behavior and I was too embarrassed to hang out with them. I can count on the fingers of one hand the people I was still in connection with. They were waiting for me to sort myself out but being with Rik they didn't want to know me and what with me being on heroin and stuff. Rik still lives like this, still has his hoarding issue.

I'm trying not to be with him. This is why I'm in Thailand now. If I go back I'll end up back with him and start moving in the same circles, the druggie circles. It's difficult though because I do love him and it's not because of the drugs that I want to be with him.

He might be an addict but he really tried to help me with my drinking. Once when I was drunk he filmed me getting violent and I thought 'Oh my God, am I that bad?' He poured my alcohol down the drain to try and stop me drinking. He helped me, he cared about me. But I was still doing heroin and so was he.

I became agoraphobic, afraid to leave the house. My sister and I weren't speaking at this point because we had fallen out over Zak. I already knew that my sister and Zak were living together as drug partners. They both have HIV so they have that bond but it felt weird to me. I was taking a lot of crack at the time and I became paranoid and thought they were in a relationship but they weren't so I accused her. She had been my friend as well as being a sister so to lose her was hard.

It was all too much for me and I attempted suicide with a load of tablets and alcohol. After the suicide attempt I got myself a really good key worker who managed to get me on the waiting list for the best detox center in England.

I had to wait about 8 months to get in. I was happy being an addict at that time because I knew I was going to sort it out. Once I got into the clinic then I knew it would be a new start for me. In the meantime I was injecting drugs all day long, taking the dog for walks, watching films, going out for dinner every night and sleeping. I was just in this bubble for months.

The clinic had one of the highest success rates in England. I was doing really well there and getting all this stuff about my stepdad's death out because I had so much guilt about that, you know. Was it because of me pursuing the court case that he had killed himself? It was good to get to speak about my feelings and come to the realization that I was not responsible.

During my time in detox I was speaking to Rik every day on the phone. My mum knew it was a bad idea to be in contact with him. He's not a good influence on me. I went on home leave 3 and a half months into the detox and met up with him for a weekend. I thought if I had been in rehab I would be strong enough to cope with whatever Rik was doing but I was wrong. I didn't do any heroin that weekend but I had a couple of glasses of wine and some ketamine.

When I got back to the clinic they did a drug test and I failed it so they kicked me out. So I got back to London, straight back into the old life with Rik, back on heroin, using constantly within 2 weeks.

That was 2 years ago. Since that rehab and coming here to New Life it has just been one long cycle of a couple of months on heroin, trying to get off it, a couple of weeks back on it, then trying to get off it again. I tried using methadone to help me (I got that off the black market) and I'd try to use it to take myself down gradually using 40ml then 30ml and so on, just to lessen the effect of the cold turkey but I was still ill and still had to deal with coming down off it.

All the veins in my arms are gone. I was in hospital a couple of times with abscesses because of the damage I have done to them. I was running out of veins to shoot up so I started using my neck. I told my mum and said, "I need your help, I'm shooting up in my neck and if I get an abscess in my neck it will kill me."

"Come to Ireland now," she said. "Right now."

I stayed with her and Steve for 6 weeks and they helped me to detox. After that I went back to London and got a job in a café.

But I couldn't bear the loneliness. I have never been able to be alone. Then my sister went out and I knew she was going to score heroin. Within a week of leaving Mum's I was back on heroin. But I still kept the café job going. For 3 months I managed it but it was getting difficult because the weather was getting really hot and I couldn't show my arms obviously because of the track marks. I was starting to sweat by the end of the day, getting really aching legs and feeling sick. The heroin wasn't lasting long enough. I was starting to suffer withdrawal by mid-afternoon and so I had to quit. The other staff had no idea that I was an addict but I had to quit before they found out. I've always been together at some level, it's always there inside me, this sensible me. I knew that if my addiction came out it would have affected my CV. I have no police record. I have always had easy access to drugs through my boyfriend and husband which has not helped because I have never wanted this life. I don't want to be an addict. I'm always striving not to be an addict.

I heard about a monastery in Thailand called Thamkrabok monastery. It's a place where you can go and detox. I said I needed to go there. Zak paid for me to go as he had fucked me over with money so many times in the past. He had just inherited some money from his mum so he bought my air ticket to Thailand and I managed to get to Thamkrabok monastery. I just got a taxi from Bangkok airport straight to the monastery. I had told them I was coming so they were expecting me.

When you arrive they take all your possessions off you and you have to wear this red uniform in case you escape. They take the whole lot, just give you a blanket, a book and a few toiletries. You have to stay there for a minimum of 7 days. You vomit for the first 5 days to get the drugs out of your system. That's why it's known as the monastery where you vomit. Unlike most detox places you don't have to clear your system of drugs and alcohol before going.

The first vomiting session was done in front of hundreds of

children. As part of their drug education they are shown the effects of drug addiction. As we all line up over an open gulley and start spewing our guts up the children are watching, looking absolutely petrified. At first I thought it was wrong to put children through such an experience but now I actually think it's a good idea. The medicine the monks give you is what makes you vomit. It's made from herbs and it's a liquid. You can't not vomit when you take it. You do this once a day for 5 days and then after that you take the medicine in pill form. The pill doesn't make you sick.

We had to get up at 4am to sweep the leaves up then we'd go back to sleep until 7am when we had to sing the Thai national anthem. Everyone's ill and feeling shit but we have to do it. At 11am we crammed into the steam bath which helps you to detox. I swear by those steam baths. It was the best detox I have ever done. Then there was more sweeping, lunch and 3pm was vomit time. After 5 days of this we were allowed to walk around the grounds and feed the fish and see the crocodile. We could visit the caves that were within the grounds of the monastery. My favorite thing was going to listen to the monks chanting. There would be 40 or 50 monks chanting in their deep voices. It was so soothing.

I didn't sleep for a month, at least not at all for the first 2 weeks then not more than a couple of hours a night for the next 2 weeks. My legs were kicking for 7–10 days. They just wouldn't stop. When you're coming off heroin it feels as if your bones are not attached to muscles. Nothing is attached to anything – that's the feeling – so you're just shaking inside, rattling. That's what did my head in the most. It was worse than the burning pain in my esophagus caused by being sick so much. It was tough but I got better quicker because it was so extreme and hard core.

While I was in Thamkrabok monastery Zak decided he was going to come out and meet me so that we could have a 2-week holiday together in Thailand. He said he had got clean but when he arrived in Thailand he was carrying a shit load of heroin with him. Four hours after leaving the monastery we went to a hotel room and shot up. He brought enough for me to get hooked again. We headed to the south of Thailand for 3 weeks where I tried meth for the first time too.

At Thamkrabok you get a really good detox but you don't get the mental help that looks at the source of your addictive behavior. I had heard about New Life at Thamkrabok monastery so I begged Zak to get me there. I needed the head stuff, I knew that. I asked him to pay for me to go for 2 weeks. He agreed, so I did my last shot, left him and went to New Life.

I wasn't in a good state when I arrived. I looked like death warmed up but I was honest with them. They said "You got here so you have a strong will inside you that seeks help." After 2 weeks I had run out of money because Zak had only given me enough to pay for 2 weeks. But they wanted me to stay so they gave me special funding, a scholarship. I said I didn't want to be a charity case but they said "We see something in you that really wants to change." It was amazing, they believed in me and they trusted me. I started doing really well here. I did brilliantly looking at my past. I looked at my heroin issue but I didn't look at my alcohol addiction. It's like the alcoholism was hidden behind the heroin addiction.

Six weeks ago I was feeling homesick, went out and bought alcohol, had a few beers and got kicked out. Self-sabotage, that's always what I do when things are going well. If you relapse at New Life you have to leave for 15 days which I did. When I came back loads of new people had arrived and it felt very different. It helped me to re-focus and now I'm thinking about my addictions more seriously. I have looked at all parts of my addiction, not just the heroin. I now recognize how destructive my alcoholism has been. I am going to AA meetings and I have got myself a sponsor. I do a lot of mantra meditation and I'm on a raw food diet. I realize I need to start caring about what I put into my body.

I'm also looking at strategies for coping when I leave here. I'm still on scholarship too so I'm happy to be telling my story to give something back because I know that my story might be able to help somebody else.

I just want to say that however deep you think your addiction is, however low and dark it gets when the drugs seem to be taking control of you and your life, you can always go up. It doesn't have to stay at the bottom. Things can change. Don't give up and think that there is no way out because there is a way out and the way out starts inside you.

I wrote the following poem. I'd like to share it with you.

Thank You

New Life is a special place to be
I felt caged like a bird but now I can be free
Before I came I was losing the fight
But coming here I've put things right.
To be free of drugs is a wonderful feeling
Stay on the right path, no wheeling or dealing.
I feel like I'm getting my life on track
Move onwards and upwards and don't look back.
I am so very grateful to be here
Facing my demons was such a big fear
But this journey which I had to do
May seem dramatic said more than a few
But my life needed a massive change
And coming to New Life may have seemed strange
This sacred place has saved my life
If I hadn't come here I would've used a knife.
So I thank you from the bottom of my heart
For showing me the life I can now start.

Sarah's Story

I come from a middle-class English background. My father was private school educated and both of my parents studied at one of the top universities in England. That's where they met. My dad was raised as a conservative but when he was in his late teens he discovered socialism and it had a profound effect on him. He became a radical socialist and in doing so he also became the rebel of his family.

It wasn't just Dad. Both of my parents were extremely active in the world of politics. They were revolutionary socialists and after they married they moved to Newcastle to be part of 'the struggle'. That's where I was born. From the very start of my life I was being taken to rallies and demonstrations. I remember the house always being full of comrades, and I was immersed in the class war, surrounded by political activists. Whereas some people are raised Catholic or Muslim, I was raised socialist.

Our home was busy and full of a lot of love, hope and inspiration. We had our challenges, as everyone does, but my parents are wonderful people and I feel very grateful to have been raised by them.

I was educated at the local comprehensive school in Newcastle which wasn't a gentle place. I had to learn to be hard to cope with it. Although there were wonderful teachers and great opportunities, it could also be an environment of violence and anger, mostly working-class kids who didn't have much in terms of either material possessions or, perhaps, hope.

I soon learned that the best way to feel safe in a competitive and often harsh world was to be busy and achieving. From a very young age I was doing loads of after-school classes: piano, singing, drama, gymnastics, karate, swimming... constantly doing, always occupied.

I was always an A student, straight As through and through. I was terrified I would fail an exam or get a B so I would study for weeks, day in and day out, just locking myself into my room and studying. I would be in tears because I was so scared of the exams. I was terrified of failure and to me failure was getting anything less than the top mark.

When I left the comprehensive I went to drama school in Bristol. I was pleased to be at drama school. I wanted to be a star. I needed to be seen. Not only that but acting was a realm where I could cry and people would clap – so I could release emotions I'd hidden for years in order to seem 'tough' and 'competent' on the outside. After drama school I had to do a showcase. You go to London and do a live show in front of all these agents. I was in a very good head space and I gave the performance of a lifetime so I immediately got an agent.

I became very successful. I was sought after and so I always had work. I loved being an actress. I had the lead role in a West End musical and also the lead in an award-winning film playing opposite one of England's most famous actors. Interestingly I played a lot of traumatized characters and rough roles, which is so unlike the real me who is a polite middle-class English girl. I understand that all the stuff that came out on stage was my shadow. That's why I could play those characters so well. The work was rolling in and I was earning a lot. It was like the Universe was throwing money at me. I was earning so much that I soon had a load of money in the bank.

Looking back I believe I then went into self-sabotage. I got terrified and I thought 'This is so amazing that it can't possibly last.' I had a short period with no work and decided that I was going to 'jump into the fire before anyone pushed me', i.e. make my life hard before life could do that to me – at least I felt in control that way. I lost faith in myself but then thought I would take back control by teaching drama so I did and very soon I was successful at that too.

But I was miserable because my heart wasn't in it. I started to feel tired all the time. I kept feeling as if I hadn't had enough sleep and my body felt really heavy. Some days I felt horrendous. My body was lead and my head was all foggy. It was like there was a wall between me and life itself. I was cut off from feeling. I was depressed. I couldn't experience life. In short, I was falling apart.

I believed I could still control this though and thought that if I got enough sleep then I would be able to stop this heavy, tired feeling. It became a kind of OCD. I now understand that I was suffering from post-traumatic stress disorder (PTSD). That means that things can trigger panic response in my body. That's what the heaviness thing was. It was my body going into freeze mode. My body was trying to do what a mouse does when it's in the mouth of a cat and 'plays dead'.

Even though I felt awful I was unkind and hard on myself and would say, 'No, I will drive on through. I have failed in sleep. It's my fault so I'm going to have to pretend to the world that I'm okay today.' Again – this thought process was a way to convince myself I was in control of these horrendous body sensations.

It wasn't long before I became an insomniac.

My obsession with sleep came, at its source, from the mind; a thought. I imagine that many people with OCD are suffering from post-traumatic stress disorder as well as OCD. It goes like this. They try to understand why they are experiencing a feeling of panic so they make up reasons and, therefore, ways to control it. They say, 'I know why I'm feeling like this. It's because I didn't flick the light switch on and off ten times.' So they flick the switch ten times and the switch in their head goes 'Okay, I have done that' and then the thought in their head goes 'Okay' and then their body goes 'phew' and relaxes.

That's what I was doing. I would look at the clock when I woke up, realize that I hadn't had 8 hours' sleep so my body would go into panic and freeze and I would have this feeling of heaviness all day. But when I woke up and saw that I had slept for 8 hours I would think 'Great, perfect, I feel really good today' and I would feel that way all day.

When the sleep issue came along, the more I tried to sleep, the more I got insomnia. It was hell. I was falling into despair. My boyfriend said I needed to get help because I would be calling him at 2am in floods of tears saying I couldn't sleep. I didn't want to seek help because I was reluctant to say that I couldn't deal with this on my own. It took me a year or two of the horrendous sleep problems before I felt ready to seek the help I needed.

One day I woke up and saw that I had only had 7 hours' sleep so I felt awful, I felt as if I wanted to die, my body felt leaden. I went downstairs, looked at the kitchen clock and realized the clock upstairs was wrong and I had actually had 8 hours' sleep. So my mind went 'ding' and immediately I felt fine. I had slept for 8 hours. All the heaviness left me in an instant. It was in that moment that I realized that my problem was in my mind, in my thoughts and so I was ready to seek help.

My friend was in a 12-step recovery program for relationship issues and she suggested that I found a 12 step for workaholics. One night when I was awake I googled workaholics anonymous and found a group. There are all sorts of 12-step programs, ones for gambling, drugs, eating disorders, compulsive spending, gambling, underearners anonymous and more. They're the same 12 steps in each group. One of the first steps you have to take is surrender to a Higher Power. I mean, the mention of anything Divine in my house was a no-no. Marx said religion was the opium of the masses and I'd always believed God was 'bad' because believing in Him kept people docile and apathetic. I'm amazed at how easy I found it to accept the idea of a Higher Power when I discovered 12-step recovery though.

At the workaholics anonymous group I was relieved to find people who understood me, who could support me. That's when my life really started to change. Up until that point I had been managing my life through the use of coping mechanisms: when to eat to feel better, when to flirt with my boyfriend to feel better, when to deprive myself of food to feel better, when to work to feel better. All of this was in place to run from feelings. I began to surrender the coping mechanisms and to allow the pain that was underneath it all to come to the surface. Very quickly I went into a food recovery group as well. At about this time my relationship began to disintegrate so then I started exploring relationship fellowships too.

Mindfulness became a part of my life at this time because 12 steps encourages meditation. It is a hugely valuable tool to me because it allows me to witness my thoughts and see when they're lying! I can also find peace without having to 'do' or achieve something first.

Then I began to experience a lot of synchronicities around work. I had two jobs going at that time. My 'A' job was acting and my 'B' job was teaching. I honestly don't know why I carried on teaching. I didn't need to make money. I had loads in the bank yet there I was earning 60 quid a day doing a job I hated. When my sister came back from the States at Christmas we had all these interesting conversations. She was teaching me about the law of attraction and that gave me the strength to give up some of my teaching.

There was definitely an issue around 'keeping up appearances' which related back to the way I saw 'being a good socialist' in my mind. My brain would tell me I had it easy, being picked up by a taxi and taken to work, always plenty of work and plenty of money but I wasn't part of the struggle. This seemed shameful to me; I had to be struggling to be 'doing my bit to help the world'. If I wasn't taking some of the shit for the comrades then there was more for them to deal with. The 12 steps helped me to let go of that need to be struggling as I saw that, for me, it was very unloving and, actually, didn't help anyone.

I was doing my relationship recovery in earnest and, eventually, my relationship fell apart because I was changing as a person.

Even though I was sharing my pain with others in 12 steps and letting them see it, it became apparent to me that the real depth of my lack of functioning and my terror I didn't show to anyone, not even my sister or my sponsor. This went on for a year. Towards the end of that year I got an acting job in New York. It was a stage role and basically I did it 100 times in a very short time, several times a day for weeks. The message of the role I was playing was 'what you need is inside you, not outside of you'. The Universe was certainly trying to drum that message home!

Although I had made great strides in healing my workaholism, insomnia and 'sleep obsession' was still an issue. This was my last place of controlling. One day I was watching TV in New York and there was this American therapist on and I remember thinking 'Oh, I would really like to have some therapy.' I even had the number of a sleep therapist in my bag. Someone at the workaholic group had given it to me years earlier but I had never called them. After that New York job I took the message on board and called him. He gave me a sleep plan. It was the most violent feeling of withdrawal I have ever experienced. When I had gone into relationship recovery I had to set my 'bottom lines', e.g. I'm not going to call him every day, I'm not going to dress provocatively or I'm not going to manipulate. They told us we would go through withdrawal but I didn't. That's because my primary issue was the sleep issue, not the relationship one.

The sleep plan was strict. I was not allowed to sleep at all during the day, not even a short nap. I could go to bed when I wanted but I had to get up at 7am. Even if I was tired, I had to get up. So if I went to bed at 12pm I had to get up at 7am. I could go to bed at 2am or 4am but I still had to get up at 7am.

This time I was dealing with my primary coping mechanism and it hurt! My sister and my sponsor knew a lot of what I was going through. My sponsor is one of the members of the workaholic group who takes you under their wing and looks out for you. In all of these times that I was obsessing over not getting enough sleep, I was always getting between 6 and 9 hours. It was all in my head, what I needed to get and wasn't getting. My sleep therapist told me I was sleeping fine but I couldn't find the words to tell him that even though I was getting sleep, I still felt exhausted.

Then finally I got on the list for psychotherapy. The doctor didn't assess me as being needy enough for much so I just got a trainee. She wasn't very skilled but at least it was an hour a week when I could express and be heard. I told her that I had a couple of mornings when I had pretty much perfect sleep but I still had this heaviness. I couldn't control it. Usually it would start in my head, a kind of heavy fog that descended over me.

All my friends were getting married and I was organizing hen do's but every morning I needed an hour to purge my pain, to cry and write my feelings down. I would cry and cry and get it out. They had no idea that I had been through this process before I met up with them. I now understand that I needed to shed those tears as part of the process of un-freezing. Then I could sort of function during the day. Sometimes it was horrendous and I wouldn't be able to control my feelings and I would even start to cry on the train. I just knew I was crying all the time but I managed to hold it together enough to carry on working.

Then one day I met my friend. She mentioned that she had been to see a nutritionist and she said she had saved her life. I got on her waiting list and after 6 months I reached the top of her list, only to be told by her that she felt I needed to see an intuitive therapist, not her. She felt I needed somebody who could draw my attention to how I really felt inside – even though I was breaking down all the time the part of my psyche that said 'I'm fine, I can handle this' was so strong that a big part of me thought I was okay and would come through this without more help. Finally, though, I could acknowledge that I had depression. Despite all these tears it hadn't crossed my mind that I was depressed! As long as I could keep my breakdowns confined to the bedroom I could manage. As long as I could appear to be okay to the outside world then I was okay.

One day at the 12-step group one woman said "My doctor thinks I should go to treatment" and as soon as she said that it was like a light bulb coming on. The 12 steps help you to love yourself and by this time I had enough self-love to have the notion that I could be there for myself. I looked at myself in the mirror and the words of an ex-boyfriend came into my head: "I've got you and I'm not going to let you go this time."

I made the decision that I was going to treatment. I just knew it was what I needed and I had money in the bank so I could afford it. I had some friends who had been to a trauma clinic and they said it was very good but then I thought, 'Well, that's no good for me because I don't have trauma.' But when I looked at the clinic's information online I saw the photo of the founder and I realized that it was the same therapist that I had seen on TV in New York. What a synchronicity!

Within a week or two I was there. When I saw her for a consultation she was the first person who could explain why I had this feeling of heaviness. When I said to her I felt heavy she said "This is why…" She explained trauma to me. She explained flight, fight and freeze. I just wept with utter relief because I could see how everything was falling into place. It was then that for the first time in my life I was able to take myself into the 12 steps with my heaviness visible and not hidden behind a façade. I was showing the real me and not the me that I wanted to show to the outside world. My friend saw me at the meeting and she said "God, you look awful!" I said "That's because I'm not hiding how my body/emotion actually feels."

So I went to treatment and had all this semantic experience in therapy that helps your body to expel the trapped energy that it hadn't been able to do many years before – when trauma happens. The trauma is locked in the cells and stays there until it can be released. That can be forever if you don't deal with your issues. I still don't and may never know what my trauma was – people can be traumatized by events as seemingly small as dental operations.

I spent 7 months as a resident in the clinic. The experience was both horrendous and amazing. All the stuff I had locked inside me forever had to come out so that it could be healed. In the process of healing I found myself. I found my ability to feel emotions. My anger used to get caught in my throat, my shame used to overwhelm me. All my emotions used to be under control but now I can feel them. I can feel the positive emotions now because my lid had been on all emotion so I had actually been stopping myself from feeling even positive things. I had not been truly alive but now I am.

I have so much joy and capacity for love and compassion.

Graham's Story

My name is Graham and I'm 33 years old. I'm the oldest in my family. I have a younger brother and sister. My parents are still together. It must be over 40 years now so I've had quite a stable background in some ways. Mum and Dad never fight with each other but I think the family looks better from the outside. What I mean is that it appears better than it actually is. My mother had a really troubled childhood because she experienced sexual abuse and violence. She wanted to give her children the childhood she had never had and to give us the love that she had not received as a child. She tried really hard to be a good mum but the trouble is that she never dealt with her own issues so all her unresolved stuff affected the way that she brought us up. Her hang-ups and her damage got into our upbringing.

She's rigid, stuck in a rut, living the same patterns over and over. I feel for her but I also have a certain amount of resentment towards her. A lot of the psychological stuff that I have had to deal with in my life has its source in my mother and the way she behaved. That said, I had a better childhood than she had, that's for sure. She was never really violent towards us. Her childhood abuse was emotional and sexual but I know that she hasn't told us everything that happened to her when she was young. The things that she has told us up to now have been quite shocking. Although there is a bit of resentment on my part, I feel quite sorry for her and I know that she did the best that she could as a mother.

I'm a traveler. I love to travel and explore the world. I have been traveling for almost a year now, experiencing what life is like in many different countries. Recently I decided that I needed to stay put for a while. I was kind of looking for something a bit settled but I didn't want to return to a 9 to 5 job in Belgium. I'm no longer interested in doing a regular 40-hour week type of job because I've tried that and it doesn't work for me. What I was looking for was something like volunteer work or spending time living in a temple. Not long ago I was in Taiwan looking for a host family because I thought it might be quite cool to experience Taiwanese family life. That was another possibility I was exploring. I'm always exploring! While I was in a Taiwanese temple studying tai chi I met another traveler and we started corresponding. It was her who told me about New Life because she had been thinking about volunteering and she told me that here I could experience community life, sustainability, yoga, mindfulness and so on. When I looked at the New Life website I saw that everything offered was something I was interested in. I thought that the community sounded pretty awesome and when I found out that the cost was quite low I thought 'That's the place for me.'

As it happened I had already decided to go back to Thailand to visit some of the areas I had not yet explored so I had my flight to Chiang Rai already booked. Chiang Rai, in the north of Thailand, is the nearest town to the community. Obviously I thought I'd check the place out while I was in the area and that's what I did and that's why I'm here. I have been here for 7 weeks. I'm not sure how long I'll stay. I'll see how it goes.

People sometimes ask me how I can afford to travel the world without a 'proper' job and I always have to explain to them that I worked for several years in a well-paid job back in Belgium, doing overtime whenever I could and so I had managed to save up quite a lot of money. Also, although I was working, a lot of the time I was really depressed so I didn't go out. I just stayed home in the evenings. That meant I wasn't spending much money, especially as I was living with my parents. My outgoings were very low so I just saved up a load of money. But even now I work as I travel to top up my funds.

I used to suffer from depression as a teenager. I think it was because I was heading down the wrong path and it was getting me down, I wasn't doing what I really wanted but I wasn't aware of that at the time. It was fear that stopped me from living from the heart and doing what I really wanted to do. I was using drugs quite a lot, especially cocaine and amphetamines. I guess they were to compensate for the fact that I was living a life that wasn't right for me. The funny thing is that even when I was using drugs I never took paracetamol because I thought they were bad for you so in the week I was very healthy and at the weekends my lifestyle was really unhealthy! I took lots of amphetamines and they did a lot of damage because I was taking so many of them. They're uppers but actually they had the effect of making me depressed and very socially anxious. I already had the tendency to be anxious and the drugs just exacerbated it.

I didn't do cannabis very much because when I tried it I would get really self-conscious and closed off so that wasn't a very pleasant experience. I seem to be particularly sensitive to it because smoking it had a very powerful effect on me, almost like tripping. I used a water pipe and rolled joints and ate it but however I took it, it always had the same effect.

I came here to New Life as a volunteer. I did consider doing the residents' program but I thought I wasn't really suffering enough, not compared to some of the people who come here who have had to deal with much more than me. At the time I arrived

I was doing relatively well. My depression had more or less gone because by this time I was living a life that suited me. I'm interested in the use of mindfulness for the treatment of depression. I thought that simply being here would help me to work on the mindfulness aspect and that's what has happened. I have so many opportunities to practice mindfulness here.

My big thing was always social anxiety and here I have had to learn how to speak up in group. We have a weekly meeting for anyone who suffers from social anxiety which is very helpful. From the very start it felt very safe to express myself in this group. There are only a few people who attend and we all have the same issue so we are very supportive of each other.

I have had some life-coaching sessions because even as a volunteer the life coaches are available to guide and support us. One of the coaches uses the Enneagram and that has really helped me. At first I was skeptical about it because I thought 'Oh, it's another personality type thing' but then I borrowed a book about it from one of the life coaches and once I identified my type it gave me a much better understanding of why I am the way I am. It showed me the way I think and act, what challenges I have to overcome and it has given me a better understanding of what motivates me. I already knew what struggles I had and what situations I found challenging but the Enneagram kind of brought everything together for me.

I'm a number 9 which makes me oversensitive to criticism. I find myself being judged and misunderstood for being too placid and indecisive. My tendency is to care too much about what other people think of me. Nine is the peacemaker, the mediator. My struggle is to know what my needs are. I forget about myself because I'm too focused on seeing to other people's needs, making sure they feel comfortable and have everything they need. In doing this, my own needs are put to one side. But even when I know my own needs it's then hard for me to communicate them to others. I feel that by speaking up and asking for what I want I'm disturbing the peace. I'm working on getting in touch with my own needs here and learning how to communicate those needs to others. It's not easy for me to do that. That's something I need to do a lot of work on.

I'm not Buddhist but I'm interested in Buddhism and Taoism. I don't attach a label of a particular religion to myself. I pick things from here and there, from various spiritual traditions. I also try and meditate but I lack some discipline. Sometimes I really feel the need to meditate, so then I do it. And of course there are the group meditations here in the community. I find it helpful for relaxing. It calms me down and I can observe my patterns but I'm not disciplined enough, that's the problem.

Anxiety has been a big issue throughout my life. It stopped me from doing a lot of things and probably led me to using drugs because some drugs – not all – make it a bit easier to socialize. My anxious nature stopped me from making positive choices in life. My heart would say 'Go there' but I was too fearful. Also I wasn't happy at school so people would say "Well, why don't you change schools? That's what most people would do" but underneath the issue is to do with communicating my needs. People would ask me to explain myself, to try and get me to say why I wanted to change but I couldn't speak up for myself. Anyway, even if I had spoken up then I would have to deal with the realities of changing schools and all the anxiety that would go with that.

I didn't go to university. I studied to be a car mechanic at trade school which was probably the biggest mistake of my life. My marks at school were high and I could have got a place at university but in my family I followed the male role models around me and that's not the route they took. My role models were all in practical trades, not professions.

I regretted that decision for a long time because I would have been surrounded by my type of people if I had gone on to study at university. In the trade school I was surrounded by guys who gained respect by being the strongest or the most macho. Somehow I survived and I wasn't bullied. Maybe that's because at some point I did become quite hard and I would fight the other guys, but acting in that way was probably part of the depression because in doing so I wasn't being true to myself. I was trying to be hard like the other guys but I'm not that type of guy.

So there I was, living a life that suited my family but it didn't suit me. My dad worked in the car industry so he was happy to see me in a similar trade. All my family are either in the trades, work in shops, as car mechanics or they inhabit the criminal world. Two of my uncles were criminals but they have both died now.

One uncle died when I was 11. He was a drug dealer and a heroin addict and he committed suicide. He was an important role model to me during my early years and I was often compared to him because physically we look alike. He was quite a soft and sensitive person but he couldn't really deal with his childhood and other life challenges, maybe because of his extreme sensitivity. Also, he really wanted to get clean but to get off heroin he had to talk about his past with the clinical therapists. One day he rang my mother from the psychiatric clinic and said to her "I'm sorry but I can't talk about these things." He had a psychotic episode and it all got too much for him and he escaped from the clinic and hung himself.

My other uncle was a professional criminal, a big drug dealer and a hitman. He had spent time in prison for murder. He did many bad things but he was a good friend of mine right up to his death 2 years ago. He was only 49 when he died from lung cancer. He had smoked heroin and crack so maybe that's what affected his lungs. Like my other uncle he was also a heroin addict and he wanted to get off heroin. He was a hard and tough man. He was loved and liked within the family but he was feared by many others. He was all the cousins' favorite uncle and he became a good friend of mine later on in life. He has also been a role model for me, more than I previously realized which no doubt played a part in some of my life choices.

These uncles were my mum's brothers who had the same upbringing as my mum. It's amazing that my mum didn't get into the drug scene too.

For a long time now I have not taken drugs like cocaine and mushrooms but I'm interested in the spiritual aspect of ayahuasca. I took it only once and it was just a small dose because I was still in my social anxiety and I held back the dosage through fear. Even so, the experience was quite enlightening and I would like to explore the possibilities of this drug further. It was a much more interesting experience than other psychedelics that I have taken. Maybe there's a benefit to that particular drug? I know that in the Amazon the tribes take it to get insights into themselves and into life, the meaning of the Universe and all that. But I like my life now so maybe there is no point in taking any drugs...

When I was younger I was living a life I didn't enjoy so I kind of balanced it out by getting out of my head on weekends but not during the week. Now I would say that I pretty much enjoy every day and just about every day is fulfilling. I used to just live for the weekends but now I don't need the ups and downs that drugs give you. I include alcohol in that statement. In fact I would say that alcohol is much more of a drug than psychedelic mushrooms.

The boss in my job in Belgium would like me to go back to my old job and I could earn a lot of money if I went but I don't want to go back to that life so I'm not going back. I don't have any plans as such. I'm taking each day as it comes. I know that I'm going to take away a lot from this place. I have really moved on in my short time here.

My advice to anyone would be to follow your heart and don't let fear hold you back. It was social anxiety that stopped me from following my heart when I was younger. Fear was at the root of it. At times my social anxiety was so great that I couldn't even walk into a supermarket or go to a party. I would make excuses, say I was ill rather than have to face my fear. Not any longer!

How to stop feeling fearful? That's a hard one. Firstly for me was to stop using drugs but then I was still in a boring job so I'd say don't stay in a job you don't like. And change the people you hang out with because they can influence you so much.

When you start to follow your heart you become more confident. Then you will be ready for exposure, exposing yourself to the things that you fear. I don't mean exposing yourself to something you cannot manage but to gradually work up to that. So for me it would be to speak up in a small group, then in a larger group, just doing a bit at a time until I will be able to speak up in front of a lot of people. To speak up in the group is a massive challenge but each time I do speak up then it gets easier.

Being vulnerable helps – just be open about it, say what your fears are, what challenges you are facing. Here in the social anxiety group I was able to do that for the first time ever. I could say exactly how I felt and nobody challenged or judged me. It's fantastic because talking about your secret fears is so liberating. Once they're out in the open they lose their power. I don't know anywhere else where I would have the opportunity to do that.

I wasn't an addict because I would only really use on the weekends but if people ask me about it I say my drug taking was definitely a problem because I couldn't stop doing drugs and it was making me more and more depressed. I would be doing mushroom trips with my friends at the weekends and be inhabiting this world of universal laws thanks to the drugs. Then on the Monday morning I would be back at work and everyone would be talking about mundane things like TV shows and cars and it all felt so surreal. Despite the fact that I was taking all these amphetamines I managed to hold down my job. But I was only just holding it together. I knew I was getting a bit close to the edge. I had to retreat to the toilets at work because I felt as if I was about to collapse. I didn't collapse or break down at work but I was getting close to it. I knew I had to make some big changes or I would have some sort of breakdown.

Psychedelics had a big impact on me at this time because they gave me insights, showed me that I was on the path of self-destruction. That made me think that if I was to destroy myself I might as well just ignore my fears and do what I wanted to do, a kind of 'nothing to lose' attitude. I began thinking that I could just ignore my fears and do exactly what I want to do so why not stop my job? If it doesn't work out, it doesn't work out but at least I'll have tried. Thinking along those lines really helped me to make the changes.

Looking back, I understand that being a number 9 in the Enneagram meant that I felt I needed to have all my reasons and excuses ready. I got myself prepared for all the questions that I thought people might ask me, as if I needed to justify my decision to give up my job and go traveling, things like:

- How will you finance it?
- Is it safe in Taiwan?
- What will you do when you come back?
- Won't you miss your family?
- What about the future?

Because I felt I had to have all the answers ready it took quite a long time for me to make the change but now I realize that I don't have to justify my decisions. I don't have to explain my choices. This is my life and what I'm doing isn't harming anyone and I'm doing much better now than I was when I was a 9 to 5 worker. My depression has lifted and that has given me confidence, knowing that I have made good choices that have improved my life. Not every single choice has been the best I could have made but overall I have done well and that has helped with my anxiety.

It might sound like a strange thing to say but I'm actually thankful that I used to be depressed. I'm grateful that I have experienced all the suffering. Without having had those struggles, I wouldn't have made the choices that I have made that have led me to having the life I have. These days I have so much freedom. I'm following my heart and doing things that I love. I'm meeting like-minded and inspiring people. I really love my life!

You see, if I hadn't been really depressed then maybe I would still be living a life which was kind of okay but I wouldn't have been happy. I would have been living a mediocre life, making do, a half life. Looking back I can see that I was just existing day to day with no joy in my world. I was just doing the same job, living in the same town and hanging out with the same people. That life wasn't fulfilling so through suffering I was led in another direction. The suffering became so extreme that I was forced to change. It was change or go under. Most people I know are not particularly happy. Again, without having experienced the real lows then I'm sure I wouldn't appreciate the feelings of happiness that I now experience on a regular basis.

Age 16–21 were the worst years for me. At the age of 21 I started seeing a psychotherapist because I was struggling to get off the drugs. I knew I needed professional help with my issues.

It was at this time that I met my girlfriend. We met at a workshop and we connected because she, like me, was in the midst of a period of transition and had started dealing with some of her issues. She wanted to go traveling so I made the decision to give up my job and go to Bali with her. I gave up a lot of things to go traveling with her but in the end it was a good decision because without her I wouldn't have had the courage to take such a radical step. It freed me. She had traveled before which was very helpful to me. I would never have had the courage to step out into the world alone but with her to help and support me I felt safe. Also it took me away from my old friends who were doing drugs. In the end the relationship didn't work out. It wasn't a healthy relationship but I don't regret it.

I was studying psychology when I met her. I was going to do a 5-year course. I had finished the first year but I was spending so much time with my head in a book and being alone in my room studying and reading that I thought, 'Do I really want to be doing this for 5 years?' I decided I didn't want to do that, that it wasn't the right path for me. Maybe I just wanted to prove to myself that I could do it. Now that I have tried the academic life I know I don't want that. I thought 'No, I want to travel and not go to university' even though I now have the qualifications to do a degree.

I am grateful that I met my girlfriend because if I hadn't I wouldn't have been here in Asia traveling, being here at New Life, meeting such interesting people. The openness, the non-judgment, the total acceptance of all parts of oneself that I receive here have opened my eyes to a new way of being.

I have all kinds of ideas of what I could do but I'm not rushing into anything. I'm being much more mindful these days. There's plenty of opportunity to practice mindfulness while living in community. I like community life and I also like to help people. I'm not depressed anymore, that's the best thing!

Hugo's Story

My name is Hugo and I was born in Belgium although I am now living in Ibiza. I am married and I'm the father of a wonderful little girl called Estelle. She is 3 years old.

I am the fifth child of five. I have two brothers and two sisters. I also have a stepbrother and sister from my stepfather's previous marriage. I come from a wealthy family and I have never wanted for anything materially.

My parents divorced when I was 3 and my mother remarried when I was around 5. I was brought up by nannies and educated by private teachers and later I went to a private school. I do not remember a lot about my childhood except that at school I was not at the top of the class and from time to time I was bullied because I was a French-speaking child in the Dutch part of Belgium so I didn't really fit in. Even with my friends I was never really accepted, or at least that's the feeling I have always had.

I was a self-contained and imaginative child. I could play for hours alone in the garden. When I became older I used to do most things on my own, even traveling to school by train unaccompanied from a young age. My parents never came to watch me taking part in any activities, nor did they attend parents' days etc. I would say that they were not very present in my daily life.

The first time I drank was when I was 14. It was at my sister's wedding. I went around drinking all the leftovers. At around 15–16 years I started to binge drink at the weekends with friends. Later, at university I began taking drugs but I didn't really get heavily into them. For me, alcohol was my drug.

I got arrested for drunk driving at the age of 18 but I only got a fine so I didn't really mind. Then after university I started working and it was then that I had my first two car crashes caused by drunk driving. Again there were no consequences. I wasn't sent to jail or anything.

At about the age of 23 I stopped taking drugs but I continued drinking. I was quite a controlled drinker because I did not drink every day.

At 25 I got married but it only lasted for 2 years and then we separated.

I was successful at work and I quite enjoyed my job. I was promoted to a new job in Luxembourg but started drinking with my boss and colleagues after work, drinking far too much. Drinking was becoming a major part of my life. I left that job after another drunken car crash and returned to Belgium.

Despite the drinking, I still managed do everything very well but I had started lying and manipulating. I began missing days off work due to my awful hangovers. I even started trying to organize my meetings around my drinking but nobody was aware that this is what I was doing.

By this time I had already had one or two girlfriends who had left me because of my drinking but I thought 'What do they know? I'm okay. Everybody gets drunk from time to time.'

Then 6 years ago I met my wife in Ibiza. For the first year we only saw each other at the weekends. During the week when I wasn't seeing her I went out drinking with friends. I drank during the day and in the evenings at the weekends. I think the real reason I was drinking was to help me to relax.

I married my wife but the drinking continued. In my eyes I had the alcohol under control. When she was 6 months pregnant I started drinking more, during the day and in the mornings too. By this time the alcohol was really taking hold. Each time I had a drink I would say that this would be the last time I would drink. I wasn't a nice person when I was drunk. All my feelings would come out under the influence of alcohol, especially anger. I have problems with low self-esteem and my wife is a very strong person and she was getting fed up with me. A few months after the birth of my daughter my wife told me to do something about my drinking. So I went to AA and tried to stop drinking and I thought everything would be okay. But AA doesn't work that way. You have to actually do the program and make the changes, not just sit there in the group.

After the 12 steps failed I went to rehab for the first time. I stayed for 5 weeks and then I was clean for about a year. This was a very nice year where I started enjoying life, enjoying my daughter and playing sports. When I went to parties I was very shy in the beginning, but even that started getting better. I always went home early when everybody was starting to become drunk. My wife used to stay later than me. Even though I wasn't drinking, I still had my deeper inner problems. During that period I was taking Antibuse and seeing a counselor in an effort to control my drinking.

I couldn't drink while I was taking Antibuse so I started

taking drugs again. I guess they were a replacement for the alcohol. But then I stopped going to AA meetings and seeing my counselor. The worst day of my relapse was the day after my wife's birthday. She said "Why not have a glass of wine?" so stupidly I drank two glasses of wine. Then we drove to a friend's house and I drank some vodka in the kitchen while the others were swimming in the pool.

When we drove back home I was very drunk and had a fight with my wife. She hit me while I had my daughter in my arms and my daughter started crying and shouting. I will never forget that image. It still haunts me.

That summer I took my wife and daughter to the Belgian seaside with my parents but I forgot to take my toilet bag with my Antibuse in it. So after a few days at the seaside drinking and doing lots of drugs, I dropped my wife at the shops and went back home to pick up something. On the way home I bought a bottle of vodka and drank some. She saw it and she was very angry. After lunch I went back home with my daughter for a nap and drank some more. When my wife came back home she was out of her mind. My brother and sister had to calm her down and we drove back to my parents' place without speaking and then returned to Ibiza. After a few days the dust settled and things were okay for about a month. Then I relapsed again. This time I was sitting in the car and drinking by myself. I drank so much that I had to be taken into hospital for 3 days to detox. When my parents heard I was in hospital they came to Ibiza to support me and stayed a week. All went well for a few weeks but I ended up back in hospital after another drinking bout. I just couldn't stop. I couldn't kick the habit.

I tried 6 weeks in a Swiss rehab clinic but when I came out I relapsed immediately. My wife was getting so fed up with me that she kicked me out of the house and I had to rent an apartment. She started using a breathalizer to find out whether I had been drinking or not. One morning she found that I had 0.01

of alcohol in my blood. She knew I had been drinking even though it was at a low level. In the evenings I used to calculate how many hours I had before going to see her so that there was time to get the alcohol out of my blood, but this time I miscalculated. She wouldn't let me take my daughter to nursery school and I was really upset.

I got drunk and took some benzos (a prescription drug). I tried to call my wife several times but she did not answer. Not that I remember much about what happened because I was totally out of it. After that incident she refused to let me see my daughter at all. She also called her mother and told her she wanted to go back home for a while because she could not handle me. Her mother called my mother and suggested that I should go back to Belgium for a few months. I didn't think this was a good idea as I could do nothing in Belgium.

Then I spoke to a friend of NA in Belgium and she told me about a very good rehab in South Africa so I decided to go there for 3 months. It was a small secondary rehab with a maximum of 12 patients. It was the best place I had been to. They spoke a lot about mindfulness and we had to work the 12 steps with a sponsor. We were allowed to go out from time to time (movies, restaurant, shopping) but always with a minimum group size of three people.

When I was there I began to understand that the source of my drinking lay with my deeper problems. It was about that time that I came across New Life on the internet and I thought it looked really interesting. I spoke with my counselor in South Africa who told me that it was not a good idea to go to another place and that I had to continue the program I had started with them. So I went to a sober living house for 3 more months where I was introduced to lots of theory about mindfulness, CBT etc. Despite all that information I felt that I was not changing in myself. I still suffered from low self-esteem and codependency. So I decided that when my 3 months in rehab were finished I was going to go to NLF in Thailand.

On the 25th of December I came to NLF and this is the best decision I have ever made. I would like to share with you some of my daily journal. I hope this will show you how a life can change in quite a short space of time.

Hugo's Diary

Wednesday 25th December 2013
I arrived in New Life on Xmas Day. I was shown to my room where I unpacked, read a bit, looked at the rules and had a rest. Today was a special day because of Christmas so we were free.

At 4pm I was shown around the place by a volunteer who has been traveling in Asia for 9 years.

At 6:30pm we had dinner and afterwards there was a movie in the forest hall but I didn't go. I went back to my room and tried to read a book but felt asleep after one page.

Thursday 26th December
I had a restless night, probably due to jet lag. I woke up around 3:30am as it was quite cold in the room and the bed was rock hard. I decided to start writing a daily journal. Around 5am I started to fall asleep again but at 5:45am the wake-up gong sounded. It's to wake up those who want to go to yoga or meditation. We must go at least five times a week. I didn't go. I stayed in bed until my alarm went at 6:30am.

During breakfast no one can speak. The reason for this is that some people with behavioral and/or sleep problems can be in a bad mood and start to complain and moan. That's not a good note on which to start the day. So we learn to enjoy and appreciate the morning and the food on our plate in silence. For breakfast we have cereals with milk and yogurt from our own cow and eggs from our ducks and all different fruits that are grown by the community.

At 8am each day we have a community meeting where everybody has to be present. Here we discuss any problems and pass on any needed information. Then we are each given our duties and work for the day.

Today I attended a self-supporting group for addicts. Of the 50 people here at the moment, 8 of us have addiction issues. The others are visitors or volunteers or people with other problems such as anxiety or depression.

At noon we had lunch with lots of vegetables from the garden followed by a movie about shame. This was very interesting for me. I have a lot of shame because of my insecurity and low self-esteem. This is very different to guilt. Shame is something you feel about yourself, like not being good enough and guilt is about something you feel you did wrong.

On the way back to our rooms a few of us were given a random drug/alcohol test. This happens regularly. I was okay because I have not taken any alcohol or drugs since arriving here.

At 4pm we had an hour of sitting meditation followed by walking meditation.

From 5pm onwards the sessions are not obligatory and you can do what you want. You are free to go to the shops or for a massage or just relax. You're not locked in. I like that because it shows they trust you.

At 6:30pm we had dinner with salad and vegetables and after that I went to a session about anxiety when speaking in public. We practiced some exercises. It was a little soft and we were not allowed to give negative feedback because it could upset some people. I do not agree. I think negative feedback is as important as positive feedback.

Friday 27th December
I did not sleep very well. Same story as yesterday. The alarm went off at 5:30am but I was still too tired so I woke up at 6:40am and missed yoga.

At the community meeting three people were leaving and made their goodbye speeches. Then everyone received their plan for the day. The first thing I had to do was to meet my life coach. I explained my situation to her. Most of us work with more than one coach as they each have different specialties. She told me that for the moment I have to focus on the now, on today and not in the future. I have to try not to make scenarios in my mind about everything happening around me. I have to try and relax and breathe and get in contact with my feelings.

Later on I will be doing some work with a Buddhist nun who will work with EMDR therapy to go in my past.

I had a Feldenkrais massage. It works by using slow, smooth movements to stimulate your body through your mind. I used it for my bad leg and could feel a positive change after a few hours.

In the afternoon we had a goal-setting session, things that we choose for ourselves. Things like going earlier to bed, not using the phone or computer anymore etc. My goal for this week is to focus more on my recovery and go deeper in the program.

In the evening a group of us went to the local town for the AA meeting. I felt I needed a meeting after a week of no meetings. I have had no alcohol cravings.

Saturday 28th December
At last I managed to wake up at 5:30am and get out of bed in time for yoga. It is great when you arrive at yoga because it is still dark outside and there are candles on the floor of the outdoor hall. During the yoga class the sun comes up within the mist on the valley. It is so beautiful. Then we have our silent breakfast followed by the community meeting. The residents have to work every morning. Today I had the two worst jobs, recycling the waste and cleaning all the bins and when this was finished we had to go working on the compost. First flatten a bed of old compost to add the fresh compost of last week. We had to shuffle the fresh-smelling compost (the smell makes you want to throw

up) to the other bed of compost further away.

Later in the day I went for a body massage together with pots they put on your back. It's called cupping and it sucks all the toxins away. My back is covered with red marks from those pots. The local woman who does the massage is very well known. The TV even came to interview her because of her traditional massage skills.

The Feldenkrais session has really made my back and breathing feel better. Normally when I sit for meditation my back hurts but it was much better today.

Sunday 29th December

Sunday is a free day. I woke up at 7:30am. I could have woken up at 6:30am for yoga but on Sunday you are not obliged to attend. So I had a silent breakfast followed by a cycle ride around the lake. It was beautiful. We did 27km in 3 hours. We stopped at a local restaurant where they don't speak or understand English and had a delicious fish meal with herbs and garlic.

One of the residents here specializes in foraging for edible plants. He gave us a demonstration about how to discover and feel if plants are edible. I think it is like playing with mushrooms :-).

A few days ago I spoke with Estelle on Skype and it makes me feel so good that at least I can see and speak to her even though I am so far away from her.

Monday 30th December

I walked in the early morning darkness to the meditation hall for the yoga session. It was a very misty morning. I understand why it is good to take time in the morning to be silent and meditate. I could feel how I got nervous and angry with the people who arrived late and made a noise by taking their mats and meditation blocks while we were already starting to meditate in silence. But after a few minutes all that stress is gone and you can focus on yourself and your day. I am sure that without the yoga and silent breakfast half the people would be complaining during breakfast about what's not okay. Now you just eat in peace with yourself and after breakfast all those thoughts are gone. Even during yoga it is amazing how fast you stop thinking about things in the past or in the future and you just start to focus on the now. You just focus on your body and your breathing.

In the afternoon we had a group therapy session. It is illuminating to realize how fast you can start seeing things in a different way and how you can find positive solutions to problems and how anger can be transformed into positivity and calmness.

In the social anxiety session I had to give my opinion on abortion and defend my point of view when challenged in front of a group.

It is so interesting to be with all these people here because you can learn so much. On my way back from the session a few of us discussed what it was like to suffer with anxiety and low self-esteem. It all comes down to the same thing. We have to become ourselves and do what we feel we want to do and not what other people or society expects us to do. You can only give love and kindness if you have it within you. You cannot give what you don't have.

Unfortunately today our society is a society of materialism, money and power and this makes a lot of people unhappy. A lot of people are not following their hearts and even though they might have everything they desire on the material level, they are not happy within themselves.

I hope I will find what I want to do with my life even if it does not provide me with loads of money and material objects. I hope I will have the opportunity to give as much as I receive. (These are my words that are coming through my mind and not from a book or lecture.) I just want to be happy and confident with Estelle, my family and my friends.

On the way to my room a girl asked me if I could help her. I said it depends what she needs help with. She asked me to catch a spider with a diameter of at least 10cm. I thought it would be better to call someone else who could catch it and let it out. I did not want to kill this poor animal even though it was frighteningly big. From now on I will put a towel along the gap at the bottom of my door at night and check the room for spiders before going to bed.

It's good that I am starting to adapt and beginning to get to know more of the people here.

Tuesday 31st December

I went to help to prepare the breakfast today, cutting up the pineapple, mango, banana and watermelon. Also preparing the porridge and duck eggs. I have bought a lot of local fruit and vegetables that you can eat raw so instead of eating crisps and chips in the evening I eat these healthy foods.

The afternoon group session was with one of my life coaches who uses a system which includes family and ancestors. It's amazing! You make a timeline on the floor. It's written on paper and it includes your ancestors, birth, present day and your future. You start by standing on the paper at the part that represents the present moment and you describe how you feel about being there. Then you try to go to your future. When I tried that my legs became very heavy. I could hardly move them and I had to make a big effort just to get closer to the future. Once I got closer my legs and feet became all tense and I started to feel pain in my legs. I broke out in a sweat. Then I had to go back down the line and up again.

One of the guys could not go towards the future at all and his legs started to shake uncontrollably. He had to go all the way down the timeline to the part where his ancestors were and then he managed to move towards the future with the help of me and a girl.

I was very surprised that walking along a line of paper with a few words written on it could have such a powerful physical effect on me. It was such a strong effect. I still don't understand and don't know what to think about it. This group took longer than expected so I missed the meditation class and had to rush to get to the AA meeting in town on time.

There were two girls and a guy who came to the AA meeting for the first time. They are not here for addiction, burnout or anxiety. They just came to relax and find themselves. Being here and discussing their lives with us led them to think that maybe they do have a problem with alcohol. Alcoholism can arise because of anxiety, depression or other symptoms. It can also happen the other way around, that you get the symptoms because of the alcohol or drug abuse. You use the substance to feel better but it's only a short-term solution. The guy had been in treatment for 10 weeks with a counselor but he hadn't wanted to go to AA meetings because he did not really think his alcohol issue was that bad. But now he has come to the realization that he is an alcoholic. He has developed a dependency on alcohol in order to be able to cope with life.

When you first attend an AA meeting you have to confess to the rest of the group that you are an alcoholic. These people were telling me after the meeting how hard it was to speak the words "I am an alcoholic" when you first introduce yourself but they felt relieved afterwards and they all said that they will go back.

After the meeting we went to eat on the street stalls that were there for New Year. As they say here, if you can stay sober in Thailand it should be possible everywhere. They drink everywhere here.

After this we went back to NLF to celebrate New Year but I did not make it. I fell asleep while waiting for midnight.

Wednesday 1st January 2014
Today is a free day. I woke up at 7am and did some meditation. At 8am we had our silent breakfast. A lot of people stayed in bed

as they had a late night last night. It was a strange morning. New Life looked like a ghost town. Some people stayed in bed and others went back to bed after breakfast. Even with no party and alcohol some people can lie about all morning. That's not my thing ;-).

Thursday 2nd January

Another bad night. I woke up at 4:55am (maybe because I went to bed at 9:15pm last night).

During my life-coaching session we looked at my shyness and the discomfort and uncertainty I experience when I have to ask for something in a shop or ask for information in the street. It's like I'm scared of doing or taking something I want just because I'm scared of what people might think of me. It is even difficult for me to ask in a restaurant where the toilet is. I had to try to find out when that started and I found it interesting to learn that things in my childhood could have made me become like this. I have to work more on this and I have to try now to act as or do what I want.

My work today was making mud bricks to use for building houses for the community. Then I went to shower, had lunch and waited for my parents to arrive. They brought me new bed sheets. They had a guided tour around the whole place and saw the cows, ducks, fields, room etc.

After they left I attended the Feldenkrais group session followed by dinner and bed.

Friday 3rd January

I woke up at 5:30am after an agitated night. I dreamed that I drank or took drugs somewhere. I felt stuck because I was afraid to come back in case I was tested. It was in a strange place with dark shadows and dealers.

Today my job was again with the mud. We are building a little meditation park with flower beds that we plaster with mud. I felt like a kid playing with sandcastles. Estelle would have loved to help.

I went to the body scan meditation followed by a good lunch. Then we made our goals for next week. I choose to do more of what I want and not let my shyness stop me. I also have to give three things I am grateful for every day. I also have to do more practical work on my recovery and not just attend the meetings. I have to put what I learn into practice. Even so, I am starting to speak and share a lot with other people.

I had a conversation with someone who has a lot of difficulties expressing his feelings or showing emotions like me. It is good to share so openly.

At 5pm we left the AA meeting and after that I went shopping. And yes, I went into some shops and asked for information and left without buying so that I could compare the prices with other shops.

Another thing I can see that has changed is the fact that I sent an email to my parents to thank them for their visit. I know it's something small but I would never have done that before. One of the life coaches here also told me she could see a difference in me since I had arrived. I'm much more open, walking around doing things and talking to people.

In the evening I had a discussion with a Buddhist nun who had a childhood very comparable to mine. From a wealthy family, she had a lot of good things but a difficult mental life. She also loaned me a book that had helped her a lot. It's called *When Things Fall Apart* by Pema Chödrön. The nun is also a life coach and she works with REM but that's not for me at the moment. With that therapy you really need specific events in life to work on. But she said we can sit together and chat. It is really so nice how you meet so many interesting people who are all so different. There is a guy who arrived the day before me and I was telling him how you could just see on his face how much he had changed and how much calmer he was. He was full of anger before and you really could see and feel it. It made him so happy when I told him.

Today I am grateful for:

- The way I acted during my evening in town
- To be here at New Life
- To hear from people that I have changed positively

Saturday 4th January

For me it is still difficult to wake up so early. This week I did yoga most days except one day when I had to prepare breakfast. I hope I won't have to do breakfast tomorrow morning so that I can stay a little longer in bed.

Did you know when you breathe out your deep breath during yoga you get rid of the toxins that are deep in your belly which will be replaced by healthy stuff you will take during breakfast?

Today I was all over the place with my mind during yoga. It was really hard to concentrate on my body. I don't know why.

I had a nice and long chat with a Swiss guy who is here with his wife. Then we had dinner followed by a movie down at the forest hall but I did not stay till the end as I was so tired. It looked like a very nice movie about gypsies and their music.

Today I am grateful for:

- The fact that I'm becoming more confident
- My new bed sheets
- That I can sleep a little bit longer

Sunday 5th January

Sunday is a free day. I went to the local flower festival with the Buddhist nun. We discussed Buddhism and she explained lots of interesting things about Buddhism such as Buddhism is not a religion but a philosophy and Buddha is not a God. I did not know that. But for some people here in Thailand it is some kind of religion. Buddhists have many different ways of living. Some are vegetarians, some are not. They wear different clothes. It all depends on where they come from.

I had a very long conversation with a French guy who has alcohol problems. He was very interested when I explained how alcoholics act and react, that it was a sickness and what it can do to you and with you. Also how it can affect your life mentally and physically. He could relate to a lot of what I said but he hadn't realized that so many of his problems had to do with alcoholism. And he said that the shame of admitting his addiction was so hard and he really appreciated having this conversation and he thanked me for being so open about it. He also discovered when he started drinking again how fast it went from a few days of control to total loss of control and the drinking became bad so quickly. He did not know that's how it goes if we alcoholics start drinking again. He had come here for 3 days because he was not feeling very well after relationship problems but he decided to stay and canceled the rest of his trip. He gave me a book about meditation after I told him I was having some problems concentrating while I meditate. Sometimes my thoughts are running all over the place.

I had a detoxing steam bath with lemongrass and eucalyptus leaves from the garden. It felt so good. Then I spoke with Estelle and Anna on Skype. It makes me feel so happy to hear my little princess that I love so much, even if the conversation is not always long and easy. It just gives me warmth to hear her voice and hear her say "I love you." I would love to have her here with me to show her all the nice things.

Today I'm grateful for:

- Being sober
- Having enjoyed this day when I was not expecting much of it
- Still keeping my journal

Monday 6th January

Today I had a meeting with a different life coach. I was speaking about my situation, how I was always trying to please other people and how I was scared to fail. For example, if someone asks me to buy something in the shop and they don't have it, I would feel bad even though it is not my fault.

She asked me to imagine myself as a small animal in such a situation and try to see what I as a person would say to that animal. My answer was nothing because I saw myself as a tiny ant which runs away. After some time I changed my mind and saw myself as a mouse. It still runs away but you can catch it in a corner and then try to calm it down. This was already a positive evolution in a very short time.

For homework I have to write how or what I feel and what I want. This is not easy for me to do.

After this session I went to the body scanning meditation. On my way to the hall I almost walked on a snake that came out of the grass just in front of me. I did a huge jump backwards. How scary.

At 2pm we had a group session. It is the first time I realized how the emotions of other people affect you in a group. I was feeling happy, joyful and quite confident at the start of the session. Some people who shared their feelings were a little sad or were having a difficult time. At the end I was still okay but not as positive as at the beginning. I could see that life is not always positive and certainly not if you count too much on what you want or hope.

Later we had meditation, walking meditation followed by normal meditation. I still have problems with too many thoughts. I think this also has something to do with my ADHD.

After a good dinner we watched a documentary about earthiness, the connection between you and earth. If you walk barefooted you won't be sick or have health problems anymore. I thought it was ridiculous, too simple to be real.

Today I'm grateful for:

- That I spoke with Daddy
- All the nice mails I received
- My bed!

Tuesday 7th January

Today I had singing meditation (yes, I had to sing). There was only the teacher, the manager of NLF, a girl and me. It was fun! The afternoon group was discussing mindfulness and how we see it. There are a few people who don't really like the rules here and others who don't like the jobs they have to do. We discussed the fact that a lot of residents and volunteers don't come to meditation or yoga in the morning because they don't wake up on time. Mindfulness in a community is helping each other and respecting each other. Don't judge the others. It was an agitated discussion at the end. Lots of people are scared or don't like rules. But I think with a big group like this you need rules and you have to respect them. The meeting ended quite late and we had to leave quickly for the AA meeting.

Today I'm grateful for:

- The meeting
- My new towels
- A good day

Wednesday 8th January

Today I didn't feel great and would rather just stay in my room. I have to be careful not to isolate myself. It is so easy to do so. In the afternoon we had a group session where we had to write down our life story in 10 minutes without stopping to think about it. You had to continue to write all the time and if you don't know what to write you just write. I didn't know what to write.

Then we had to underline five major events in this story and analyze them. First my life story was not really fun and all the major events were all about not feeling good enough, not feeling recognized, fear that people don't like me and abandonment.

Then we had to discuss and share this in small groups and try to find something positive in these events. For me it is that I found out that in the future I want to do something where I am in contact with people or helping people.

That evening one of the volunteers shared his life story. It was a very strong, emotional and honest share. He is a gay guy and had really had a tough life with no real love and lots of difficult times.

It is strange how people adapt fast to a lifestyle when you live somewhere. I don't shave every day anymore, I don't use after-shave, I eat chilies and fish sauce for breakfast. More and more I walk in bare feet. I don't carry my phone with me all day. And if I had just been on vacation for 2 weeks I am sure I would not have changed all my old habits. So many things happen uncon-sciously in your mind and if you are open to change they just come, you don't have to think all the time about what will happen and what other people are going to think.

One thing is sure, that I will stay here as long as I need to because this place is really doing me a lot of good. I know that if my mind and body is not well I cannot cure my sickness. If I feel good and strong I will no longer need substances to forget or push feelings or thoughts away, or to make me feel better. If I feel better the people around me will be happy and will also feel better. Now I will also have to find out what I want to do and what direction my life will take in the future. This is also a very important decision I will have to make. Because if I do something I am not happy with, that will make me unhappy and that can take me back to where I was, like a vicious circle. I see that I have destroyed a lot of things at home in Ibiza and also in Belgium…

I will have to find a new future somewhere somehow.

The advantage is that I have an open future in front of me and

I have to list all advantages against disadvantages. I have to be careful not to be lazy and go for the easy things that can bring me back where I was. Sometimes tough things are better even if they are more painful but in the long term they will be better for everybody. For sure the disadvantage is that for the moment I have no concrete plan for when I come back. Where do I go? What job? Where am I welcome?

It would be easier to know that on a certain date I would be going back home and starting work in a known place, but then that would simply be returning to the old life. At least now I have the possibility of choosing what is best. And as I said one thing is sure, if I'm well and happy then everybody around me will feel better. If I'm happy and love myself I will be able to give love and happiness to others. They say you can only give what you have. So you need to love yourself and be happy before you can give it to others.

Today I am grateful for:

- That I could write down my feelings about my future
- That I could listen to the share of a life story
- That I felt more positive at the end of the day

Thursday 9th January
This morning I woke up as usual at 5:30am and decided to go to meditation instead of yoga. The walk from my room to the forest hall was beautiful. I think it is the first time I have ever looked up and enjoyed the stars in the sky in the early morning. The sky full of stars is really impressive here. I have already enjoyed it in the evenings and have even downloaded an app to explore the stars.

We did a 20-minute meditation followed by 10 minutes of walking meditation. That was enough for me. It is not easy to stay with yourself all the time. You have to learn it little by little. My back and sitting position were feeling much better.

On my way back I took some pictures of the rising sun. It was so utterly beautiful.

This morning my life coaching session was quite intense and very emotional. I really struggle when I try thinking of my future. Instead of doing what I think is the best for me, I take too much into account what others will think or feel. In the end I have to be happy and well, otherwise I will fall back to where I was. At first I struggled with the idea of disregarding what others may want or think. Then when I started getting over this, I began to cry. It is not easy to change.

In the evening I attended the self-supporting group for addicts. It was a good group and we had a good share.

Friday 10th January
This is the prayer we read before every meal. It is really nice and it respects everything and everybody who was needed to have this food on your plate.

This food is a gift of the earth, the sky, numerous living beings and much hard work.

May we eat with mindfulness and gratitude so as to be worthy to receive it.

May we recognize and transform our unskillful state of mind, especially our greed.

May we keep our compassion alive by eating in such a way that we reduce the suffering of living beings, preserve our planet and reverse the process of global warming.

In this food we see clearly the entire Universe supporting our existence.

We should take our time as we eat, chewing slowly until the food becomes liquefied. Let us enjoy every morsel of our food. Let us establish ourselves in the present moment, eating in such a way that solidity, joy and peace be possible during the time of eating.

Upon finishing our meal, let us take a few moments to notice that we have finished, that our bowl is now empty and allow gratitude to fill us as we realize how fortunate we are to have had this nourishing food to eat, supporting us on the path of love and understanding.

In the goal-setting group I chose to continue to be more assertive and to make more of an effort to speak with people I don't know.

Two days ago I found some interesting information about Reiki classes in the city of Chiang Mai. It's 150km from here and I got the authorization from my coach to go for 10 days. I found out about it by chance. One of the guys here had been to the woman for healing because he had injured his knee. He told me how good this healer was. Like me, she is Belgian but has lived in Thailand for more than 30 years. I googled her to see if she could help with alcoholism and that's how I found out about the Reiki classes. I was curious about it and sent her an email. She replied that she can give me three sessions for my alcohol problem and after that I can begin to train as a Reiki healer.

After an intensive week of study I will receive a certificate. Then I will have to practice for a minimum of 2 months and a hundred hours before I can do the next class. What is good is that I will have the chance to practice every day with the people over here, if they allow that. She also teaches Asian bio-energetic therapy and aromatherapy. This takes more time so if I want to do this I will have to stay there. But this is not for now. So that's good news and I am very excited about this.

In the evening we went to the AA meeting. It is unbelievable how more and more people are coming with us because they start realizing that maybe they drink too much or have problems controlling their drinking. And quite a few people who have no problem but they want to stop drinking.

Saturday 11th January
As usual I woke up at 5:30am and at 5:45am I went to milk and feed

the cows and clean up their place a little. Nice, first thing in the morning to clean up cow poo! Milking went well and for the first time ever we had 5 litres of milk. I enjoy taking care of the animals.

We are all impressed how community life can be nice and although we are a big group no one fights or argues. We all depend a little on each other. Probably it also has to do with the mindfulness that we practice here.

Today I am grateful for:

- Nice conversation
- Good food
- Enjoying my day

Sunday 12th January

I am exploring the possibility of starting beekeeping here to produce our own honey. This is another thing I'm excited about. It makes me feel good to have some responsibilities. It is the same as taking care of the animals. You can't just postpone taking care of them. They need you. Anyway I like it.

I spoke with Estelle on Skype who was happy to speak with me and she wants to come to see me here and help me. It makes me feel so good when I speak with her. She is such a nice girl. That's the only thing I miss from home. And sometimes it makes me feel sad not being with her and enjoying what I am doing here with her.

Today I'm grateful for:

- The beautiful bicycle trip I did
- My massage
- To hear that my baby was happy to speak with me

Monday 13th January

Today I felt a little sad. I miss Estelle.

We had a group session where we could share our feelings. It seems as if everybody was a little down, tired. Life cannot always be positive and beautiful.

I have been looking for a hotel or place to stay in Chiang Mai. I found a couple of places for 10 euro a night. I hope they will be okay. I have not yet decided whether I should stay near the place where I have my sessions or in town so I am close to the meetings in the evenings and don't have to drive back home in the dark.

Tuesday 14th January
I had a session with one of my life coaches but I was not very impressed as she sounded negative about everything in general, even about my Reiki classes next week. I don't understand. Last week she thought it was a good idea. Maybe it is my perception of the session. The session was not really deep. Anyway, everything cannot always be positive.

We had a group session that started very slowly. We had to walk around and look at each other and then sit with a partner and go further and further away and then come closer again. The idea was to discuss the feelings that arose when someone tells you what to do. But then we had to walk blindfolded and trust the other person to guide you around. I really had problems trusting that the other person would not stop me from walking into a pillar or into the pool. Afterwards, when we shared our feelings, someone was saying that she felt like a small child trusting her mother because she could do nothing. So I shared that for me it was totally the opposite, I wanted to put my hands in front of me to see that nothing was in the way, tapping with my feet when she said "Three more steps before a step down", etc.

So the life coach told me that it is probably an old trauma about something that happened long ago and I should try to practice that particular exercise every day. But I told him that after a few days I would probably be even more mistrusting. I would be thinking that if the person leading me could see that I was doing well, she would then play a joke on me and walk me towards the pool or something else. So he told me it can be something deep. It can even be something quite small that happened but had a big effect on me. A trauma doesn't have to be a big event.

After the group we received the news that a girl was sent away because she relapsed last night. It made me sad because she had been here for quite a long time. But she was feeling too confident and had stopped attending meetings, etc.

After that I went for an hour to the meditation class which is getting better and better. It is becoming easier to stay in the now.

I also decided that I was going to put a new tattoo for Estelle on my leg over my existing one which is not nice. It will be a star with some writing.

Today I am grateful for:

- The food I had today
- That I still feel good
- To have these wonderful people around me here

Wednesday 15th January
Last night I had strange dreams, I tried to make someone stop drinking but I couldn't. Maybe that was because we heard the story of a girl who relapsed.

Today we had another group session about our inner critic. The question was 'Who would I be if I did not listen to my inner critic?'

So we had to write a story of how we saw ourselves or our life.

After that we were asked to find a symbol in nature to symbolize this. Because of Estelle (her name means star) I thought of a star. So the next thing that we had to do was to write a poem or something about that symbol. I am really no good at such things.

But the low light pollution here means that the sky at night is very beautiful. I think I already mentioned that. Also I have had a tattoo of a star on my leg. So my text was:

> Every day when I look towards the sky at night I see the stars. Being here I am so far away from you. I have never been in a place where the stars are so bright to remind me of you and make me feel a little closer to you. But this star will remind me of you on the cloudy days and you will be with me in every moment.

I think this is not too bad for me?

After this group I went to the meditation for one hour. We did it outside but it is very difficult because of the mosquitoes.

In the evening we heard the life story of our manager. I can totally relate to his story. It is almost as if he is telling my story. Maybe I should do the same as him and vow to become a monk for a few years in a monastery. He had gone to the monastery at Thamkrabok to detox and while he was there he asked a monk what he could do to become a better person. The monk told him to become a monk for as long as he had been an addict. So that's what he did. He became a monk.

Towards the end of his vow he met a rich Belgian businessman who was also at Thamkrabok monastery for addiction problems. Together they discussed the idea that there should be somewhere to go after the detox, somewhere that was run along the lines of mindfulness. So after some time the businessman sent a text to the monk to ask him if he wanted to manage and start this place. He had already bought the land. There was nothing here except an old building and a leaking pool. There was nothing growing. It was a big challenge but now he is as happy as he ever could have been. It just had to be like this. There is a good reason for the bad things that happen. Often so much good comes out of difficult experiences.

I think I am lucky that there are a few people who still believe in me and have always supported me during these horrible and difficult times. There is always light at the end of the tunnel and a positive outcome is possible. I am really lucky and thankful for this.

Thursday 16th January
Had a very agitated night with more strange dreams, probably because of last night's story.

I had a coaching session with the guy who did the test where you had to trust someone who walks with you when you are blindfolded. I had to try to remember things from my childhood and I don't remember much. My room at home was orange I think. I can't remember having breakfast or dinner. I remember the name of my nanny but not really what she looked like. I don't remember the teacher who helped me with my homework. I remember that one day I fell from a gate and had a hole in my head. Also that at school I was left on the side but not really bullied. Probably that's the reason why I could play alone for long periods. I also remembered the time when I went to the movies without telling anybody where I was going. I think I was around 7. They thought I was lost. I also remember my first yellow bike. I really could feel a lot of sadness welling up inside me but I found it very difficult to express it. Then I also felt some sadness due to not being with Estelle.

Today we also had an addiction support group. There was a new woman who is addiction counselor and she explained that one of the explanations for addiction is wanting to change or do something to your feelings, no matter the consequences. And I can totally relate to that. You try to put all your feelings away with your substitute. I drink to stop feeling my feelings because they are too uncomfortable. But drinking doesn't deal with my problems. Alcohol is not a solution.

I booked my room in Chiang Mai. It is not in town but next to the place where I will have my classes and sessions. That is safer than being in the city close to the temptations of all the bars.

The afternoon group was for everybody, all the residents, the volunteers and the guests. It was called NVC. It is a difficult subject.

Today I am grateful for:

- Being in my bed
- That I write this journal
- That I am doing well

Friday 17th January

I still have problems doing everything I want to do. I want to start organizing something but then I start thinking along the old lines. What are they going to think? Maybe they will take it personally? Why now? etc. But I will have to do it. I have to change.

This week's goals are to do at least 30 minutes of meditation every morning and to go to at least five AA meetings while I am in Chiang Mai.

The hotel is booked. The trip is booked. I have checked the times of the AA meetings. I'm excited about this!

The meeting was good. We shared the fact that most people are seeking happiness while in active addiction with their substance of choice. This is very true for me.

After the AA meeting I went for dinner at the food market and we drove back home. Everybody was breathalized and I think no one was positive.

Monday 20th January

I really understand why they have silent breakfast. This morning for sure I would have complained about one of my neighbors who was calling for half an hour on his speaker phone at 2:30am. Noble silence starts at 9:30pm until 8am the following morning. Waking people up in the middle of the night is not mindful. He is a very strange guy, spending all his free time in his room on his laptop and only coming out when he has to.

After that I had to meet my life coach and we discussed my departure for 10 days to Chiang Mai. I think I am well prepared. I have chosen a hotel out of town close to the place where I will have my lectures so there will be less temptation to go into the bars in town.

I have more and more things coming back into my memory. This is partly because after a long time of sobriety your brain starts to work normally and all the negative influences of substances start to disappear. It can take between 1 and 2 years until everything is back to normal.

We had a group session to discuss our feelings and check in.

Someone shared again something very true and interesting, how we tend to concentrate on what we cannot do or what we have to avoid doing. Firstly this puts your attention on that negative thing which can actually act as a trigger. Try not to think of a blue rabbit. And? What did you think of? It is easy to go to a place and say 'I am going to have a good dinner with a nice juice' instead of 'I am going to have dinner and I can't have a drink.' If you only concentrate on what you cannot do or have, you are stuck.

We had an hour of meditation. And I can feel how good it is to stay in the now and be nice to yourself.

Tuesday 21st January
In the community meeting I was the only one leaving. I had to say goodbye to the people I won't see anymore when I come back. I still find it difficult to express my feelings. They are there but I don't feel comfortable sharing them. I'm always thinking 'What are the others going to think?' even if it's nice things. I'm just so scared of saying something that people will think is stupid.

Today I started my Reiki in Chiang Mai. Firstly I showed the therapist a few points where I feel pain. So she says I first need

ABET (Asian biological energy therapy). They do diagnostics through acupuncture points and your energy. It is quite amazing how it works. It helps to return your energy flow to normal. I had some Reiki and cranio-sacral therapy. It took about 2 hours. After that I went to the hotel and had dinner. I went to bed early and I could feel that things were happening in me.

Wednesday 22nd January

I continued my treatment and after that I had a good lunch at the hotel and took a taxi to town to meet the tattoo guy. I described to him what I wanted and showed him some pictures. I explained it had sentimental value and had to be well done and the text is important: 'My bright star Estelle, my daughter.' It is not easy to write it down in English.

Then I went back to the hotel and early to bed. I really could feel lots of things were happening within me, even more than last night. Something is changing.

Thursday 23rd January to Sunday 26th January

I went back for my third treatment early in the morning and then had my tattoo done. The following 2 days I did not do much. A lot of feelings were coming out. I was very emotional. Lots of things were happening. It was all really strange.

I wanted to watch a movie about a father with his daughter and it was too hard for me. I had to stop it because I was getting so emotional. I have never had something like that happen before. With Reiki sometimes your symptoms can worsen because Reiki puts them into overdrive in order to combat the imbalance but this is temporary. Sometimes past illness can reappear because it was not really cured but was just suppressed. You also can feel very tired, have a runny nose and headaches etc. I had all of those this week.

Monday 27th January to Wednesday 29th January

We started the Reiki class in the morning and in the afternoon we started to practice on each other. You could just see that a lot was happening. After four patients I was shattered and I had to go to bed early.

The next day we were picked up and taken to a mental hospital for women. You cannot imagine what I saw. Women tied to their beds and living in terrible conditions. Some patients have been abandoned by their families. One of the patients I practiced on just started to cry and could not stop. You could see that she was being released of something. Afterwards she fell asleep. In total I did seven patients.

On Wednesday we went to a mental hospital for men, many of them also abandoned by their families. It was like the movie *One Flew over the Cuckoo's Nest* with Jack Nicholson.

At the end of the course I received my certificate. I went back to my teacher to pick up all the stuff I had ordered from her. She also makes her own essential oils, mosquito repellent, hydrolates against all different things such as pain, nausea etc., natural herbal medicine and her own tea from the trees in her garden. She is a very interesting person.

I returned to New Life and straight away people started asking me for treatments. I am lucky I have so many people around me to practice on. After about 100 hours of practice I can start the Reiki master course.

Monday 3rd February

Back to the routine at New Life. At 6:30am I woke up for the silent breakfast and this was followed by the community meeting. A lot of people had left during the 2 weeks I was away, including some of my good friends. But life goes on…

It is difficult to have to adapt again to following the community rules.

I asked my coaches if I could give some Reiki sessions and

they will discuss it. Anyway I can always do it privately. I have a lot of people asking if I can give them a session.

During my life coaching session I described my experiences and all the feelings and emotions that I went through during my stay in Chiang Mai. After that we spoke about my low self-esteem and the way I react, never saying what I think and not standing up for myself, always trying to please others and being scared in case I give the wrong answer or not pleasing the other person with what I do, etc. At the group session we spoke about how we feel and how we are doing. I feel positive and calm.

Tuesday 4th February

Today I worked on the fact that I have to stay in the now, in the present moment and slow down. I need to stop doing everything so fast and start being present in my activities. It is true that I eat very fast, I walk fast, everything I do has to be quick. Even when I go to the restaurant I get nervous at the end when the others want to stay a little longer.

Then we had a group about our brain accepting things from the age of one year. At that age what we see or learn we take as it has to be. It was a little difficult because we watched movies showing little children and how they react.

One of the newcomers at the AA meeting did not like the idea of presenting ourselves as alcoholics. He thinks that's in the past and now we need to look to the future. Unfortunately it is not like that. It is an evaluative sickness that always will be there. You can't cure it but you can keep it stable by not drinking.

Wednesday 5th February

After lunch I did Reiki on my first patient. She loved it and had strange feelings happening in her spine. She was all calm and happy. She even enjoyed meditation which she doesn't normally like. I also did Reiki on the cat and she looked like she had been knocked out. The girl who had Reiki asked me what I had done to the cat!

The afternoon group was about writing down without thinking about what you write down. What came out for me was that I have to become stronger for myself and to continue working on my self-esteem. I tend to give answers I don't want to give but the other person would like to hear. But now I have to start saying what I think and if the other person doesn't agree that's not my problem. Of course you have to stay reasonable and take responsibility. But up until now it has all been about what the other person might say or think. Now I have to change that pattern. It is time to do what is the best for me. I will have to do with my life the best I can do. I will make my decisions based on the way I think will be the best and not the way anyone else thinks. Of course I can always listen to advice but I don't have to do it the way they prefer. This is easier said than done. You also don't always have to listen to what your mind tells you, certainly in my situation of low self-esteem. I am so easily influenced by my mind and other aspects.

We had meditation given by the Buddhist nun. I loved it. I think I could enjoy going for a month or two to a monastery and living there as a monk.

We had a detoxing steam bath followed by the life story of one of the residents. He had suffered a lot in his childhood and adult life but he was strong and didn't give up. He said how important and empowering it was to forgive, even the hard things in life. And he said when life is difficult or you are in a depression then don't listen to your mind. He learned a lot through meditation. And he is such a nice guy now.

Thursday 6th February
I went to meditation for an hour. I can concentrate much better now. I did some Reiki on myself beforehand and gave two people distance healing. Time flies like this.

In the morning we had an addiction group that is now led by

me. It was a very good group with very deep sharing.

Then we had lunch and in the afternoon I had a Reiki patient who almost fell asleep. She enjoyed it a lot.

Tomorrow I have been told that I can announce to the group that they can have sessions with me. I will do between one and three people a day.

The afternoon session was about 'hoponopo' and it was emotionally very tiring.

Friday 7th February

It's my birthday. I hope Estelle will call me and send me something.

In the community meeting a woman from France said one thing that's very true and that is that we are very grateful to all the volunteers who work so hard for the community. They work morning and afternoon, unlike the residents who only work in the morning. The guests do not work at all. About 60% of the people here are volunteers.

I also announced that from Monday on I will give Reiki sessions. I already have a waiting list of 3 to 4 days.

I spent time chatting with some of the people. It was nice to talk with others and to notice how I am changing. I even don't take my antidepressant medicine for my anxiety anymore. And I feel very well.

April

This month I flew to Malta to see my little daughter Estelle. It was her sports day at school and she was very happy to see me. The next morning I went to help to get Estelle ready for school. Later that day I went to the AA meeting and after that I went to say good night to her.

Next morning I had more things to arrange and went to the airport with Estelle and my wife Anna. She was leaving me with Estelle while she went away. It made me feel very good that my wife Anna was happy and positive to see me and was starting to trust me again. I know it is all in my hands.

On Tuesday I brought her back to Anna. It was sad to say goodbye but I really have to do everything I can to get better forever. I really had a wonderful time with Estelle and I'm happy that everybody was positive about me. Let's continue this way.

It is so strange that before this trip I was projecting forward in a very negative way. I was stressed and anxious in the week before I left New Life. My life coach was concerned about me. She said there is no need to stress because you cannot change the future and what will happen will happen, positive or negative.

And then after all that worry and anxiety everything went so well, even better than I could ever have imagined. This gave me a lot of strength and I feel much stronger and happier inside of me. When I came back lots of people said that they could see that I changed.

This evening we had a life story of a young American guy who had a difficult childhood. He explained how he had found peace with himself by living in the moment. Of course he still encounters problems but he doesn't judge, nor does he react when people judge him. When things go wrong he laughs at himself and says 'There's no need to stress because you have it in your hands.' I felt so peaceful when I heard him telling his story. He did not mention any negative thing from in the past. He had sent loads of letters and emails to people saying that he was sorry for the way he had judged them. I still have a lot of work to get that far.

It was beautiful on my way back to my room. The moon was all red because there was a lunar eclipse.

The vibe here is very nice for the moment, a lot of Zen people and I get on well with them. Normally I am not the kind to mix very much with everybody.

I had a meeting with my other life coach and I am going to continue to work on my anxiety, fears and self-esteem.

In the afternoon we had a group about our goals for next week. Mine are to finish step 4 in AA and to start getting out of bed at 5:30am for meditation or yoga 6 days a week, including when I wake up to milk the cows.

It is amazing how much better and confident I felt after my trip to Malta. This was a good lesson for the future. This is something I have to work hard on, to accept things as they are or as they will be and to stop projecting forward. I can't change the future. If I can work on that and my self-esteem that would be very good and I could start enjoying life in a normal way. As I said before, I have to do it and will give it the time I need because I don't want to fall back this time. Not for me and not for Estelle. I want to be there for her in the future as a good father where she can count on me at any time. That is how it is in this moment.

Mindfulness

What Is Mindfulness?

It sounds like something mystical or unreachable when you hear somebody say, "I'm going on a mindfulness retreat..." or "I'm doing a course on mindfulness." Actually it's very simple. Mindfulness is the term that we use for being fully present in each moment. Let me give you a couple of examples.

Washing up without mindfulness: I'm washing up at the kitchen sink thinking about what I need to do later that morning. I have to get petrol before I go out so I'm thinking about driving to the petrol station. I must unload the washing machine and hang up the clothes when I get back. I'm thinking about my mother and wondering how she is today. I hope she remembered to take her medication. What if she forgets? Maybe I need to ring her to remind her. I think back to the last time I saw her and I recall how swollen her legs were and how she couldn't walk very well. I'm worried about her.

Washing up with mindfulness (mindfully): I can feel the heat of the water through my rubber gloves. I notice how the bubbles have a colorful slippery film on them. I can smell the lemon from the washing-up liquid. I hear the sound of the water as it trickles over the edge of the washing-up bowl. Two cups clink together. One of them has a high-pitched 'ting' and the other one clunks. I lift one of the cups out of the water and put it on the draining rack. It's a Chinese cup and it has Chinese writing on the base. I look at the writing and observe how beautiful the script is.

Walking without mindfulness: I'm walking quickly because I have to get to the station in time for the train. I'm thinking about the talk that I am giving at 6:30pm. I am imagining what it will be like to have to speak up in front of this group of people. I have not seen the hall where I will be giving the talk. I wonder how many people will turn up. What if nobody comes along? I hope the projector doesn't give out on me. Why do I illustrate my talks? Surely it would make life easier if I didn't. I hope the train will be on time. What if it's cancelled? There has been recent industrial action so that's a possibility. Then what would I do? I would have to get a taxi but there might not be one available.

Walking with mindfulness (mindfully): I walk quickly. My strides are quite long. I can hear a slight thud as my foot makes contact with the pavement. I make my strides even longer. I can feel a slight pull on the muscle on the inside of my thigh but it's not unpleasant. I notice that my breathing is slightly labored because I am walking so fast. I'm enjoying this walk. I walk past the bakers and smell the freshly baked bread. The wind brushes the side of my face.

When we are not being mindful, the mind creates lots of little scenarios. I call them the 'what-ifs'. What if this happens? What if that happens? What if she says that? These scenarios don't exist anywhere except in your mind. How can you feel peaceful and calm if your mind is busy and distracted, worrying about all these what-ifs?

The mind also has memories, re-running events that have happened in the past. Looking back and projecting forward both occupy the mind and when your mind is busy you are not fully alive and in the moment.

I keep reminding myself that the only thing that exists is the moment. Everything else is either a memory or a thought form. (Sam)

Through the practice of mindfulness I have learned not to look back at what happened or what might have been and also not to look forward at what could happen in the future. I just try and remain in the present moment and in the moment everything's okay. Everything else is just the mind affecting the peace that I know is inside me. It's inside everyone. (Julia)

A good way to become more mindful is to bring yourself into the moment using the breath. This is called breath meditation. Simply observe your breath without any thoughts. It sounds like a very simple practice. Try it right now. Just close your eyes and focus on your breathing for 2 minutes. You will discover that although it sounds very simple it can be quite difficult to do.

Why Meditate?

We meditate in order to cultivate awareness. Awareness is required to practice mindfulness. As well as breath meditation there are other meditation practices such as:

- guided meditation
- silent meditation
- listening meditation
- walking meditation
- forgiveness meditation
- meditation on compassion, loving kindness and equanimity

Thoughts are just thoughts. Feelings are just feelings. Urges are just urges. Desires are just desires. Cravings are just cravings. Emotions are just emotions. All of these come and go. They are transient. During meditation we can actually watch them come and go without getting involved in them. By learning to observe and let go we will no longer be slaves of our desires and cravings.

As our mind becomes clear and balanced there will be more space for positive and creative thinking. We also learn to relate to ourselves with kindness and acceptance as opposed to getting stuck in fear and self-loathing.

A Short Course in Mindfulness

This is a simple course in mindfulness. Try spending a week on each of the following five stages:

1. Breath

Sit comfortably or lie down on your back.

Become aware of your breathing. Feel the sensation of cool air passing through your nostrils and going down into your lungs. Feel the abdomen expand and notice how the air coming out of your nostrils is slightly warmer than the incoming air. Pay as much attention to your breathing as you can.

This is what usually happens: you focus on the first few breaths and then you might hear a sound, smell something, feel something or start thinking about something. Then you have to remember your original intention to be aware of your breathing. So gently guide your attention back to your breathing...

Feel the breath as it enters with a cool feeling and then follow it as it gently travels down into the lungs...

Then you might start worrying about dinner, or what's on TV... Catch yourself as these thoughts arise. Remember that your intention is to be aware, to be in this moment.

Put your attention back on the breath. Gently remind yourself that you are focusing on the breath. Breathe in. Breathe out.

Then you might realize that you have started thinking again. That's okay. Be patient with yourself. Guide your awareness back to your breathing.

Directly experience, feel and explore your breath *as it is* without trying to manipulate or change it. Allow your attention to rest on an aspect of the breath that you are most comfortable with, e.g. the rise and fall of the abdomen, or the air entering and leaving the nostrils.

At the end of your session spend a few moments reflecting on how it went. Thank yourself for setting aside the time to meditate.

2. Awareness

During stage 1 you will have noticed how the mind naturally wanders to other things – thoughts, feelings, body sensations or sounds. This time, when you notice this happening, acknowledge where it has gone. For example your mind may get pulled into thoughts about the future. Note it. Apply soft and gentle energy to encourage your awareness to rest on the breath. Don't try to force the mind – just encourage, with patience and kindness where possible. Your attitude is central to this practice – see if you can help your mind in a way that is healing, not violent! Don't use these practices as another means to fight and resist your inner experience but let the practice help you to 'let be' from a place of clarity and balance.

As you breathe in imagine you are bringing in energy, vitality, the life force... As you exhale, feel the body releasing toxins, stress and any negativity that has accumulated... Feel all the concerns roll off your shoulders.

At the end of your session spend a few moments reflecting on how it went. Thank yourself for setting aside the time to meditate.

3. Observation

Posture: Gently close the eyes and find your posture. This could be sitting cross-legged on the floor, sitting on a chair, sitting with your back against a wall or lying on the floor with the knees bent up. Be awake and alert but also relaxed. Feel the weight of your body, noticing where the body makes contact with the floor or the chair.

Commitment – intention: Remember your intention for being here. Commit to being present to the best of your ability during the practice. Be gently determined, knowing that you can begin again as often as you need to during the session. Release whatever your mind is occupied with. Let go of the past and the future.

Breath: Rest the attention on the breath, noticing the sensations in your abdomen as you breathe in and out. Notice the pauses in between the breaths. Simply observe your body breathing.

The sensations: Allow the breath to fade into the background of your experience. Bring the attention to the sensations in the body. There may be tingling, pulsing, throbbing, itching, pain, discomfort or pressure. Explore any sensations that you feel. If any of these sensations are particularly intense, explore them with gentle curiosity.

Sounds: Allow the sensations to fade into the background. Observe the sounds inside and outside your body. Notice the texture and pitch of the sounds.

Thoughts: Allow the sounds to fade into the background. See if you can notice the next thought that comes to your mind. Notice thoughts as they arise. You can gently label the thought as 'thought' or 'future thinking' or 'memory' and then let them go. Gently guide your attention back to your breathing.

If you get lost or overwhelmed at any point simply bring your attention back to the breath.

At the end of your session reflect on how this practice was for you today. Trust that anytime we bring mindful attention to our experience, anytime we stop and have the intention of coming to the present, we are nourishing ourselves.

4. Everything is okay
Sit or lie somewhere comfortable. Bring your attention to the breath.

Feel the breath as it enters with a cool feeling and then feel it warming up as it gently travels down into the lungs… Fill the lungs with a deep inhale, bringing in energy, vitality, the life force... As you exhale, feel the body releasing toxins, stress and any negativity that has accumulated... Feel all the concerns roll off your shoulders.

Repeat to yourself this very simple statement:

Everything is absolutely okay right now.

There is nothing you need to change in this moment, nothing to cling to, nothing to push away. You can make space for the way things are, right here, right now.

Let your attention feel the in-and-out breathing wherever you notice it, as coolness or tingling in the nose or throat, as a rising and falling of your chest or abdomen. Relax and softly rest your attention on each breath, feeling the movement in a steady, easy way. Let the breath breathe itself in any rhythm, long or short, soft or deep. As you feel each breath, concentrate and settle into its movement. Let all other sounds and sensations, thoughts and feelings continue to come and go like waves in the background. You are alive and breathing and everything is okay.

5. Loving kindness

We can cultivate loving kindness by focusing our attention on our heart.

Bring your attention to the breath. Breathe deeply into the area of your heart. Just imagine that your breath is filling the heart area with warmth. With each breath feel the warmth and the energy increasing.

Breathe in warmth and love. As you exhale imagine this warm energy flowing out into the world. Wish for all the beings in the Universe to be happy, peaceful and free from suffering. This includes *you*. Send this love out into the Universe.

Benefits of Practice

- Through regular meditation practice we become much more mindful.
- Cultivates awareness – this helps us to develop a witness stance so that rather than being lost in thoughts, feelings or emotions we are *aware* of them.
- Helps us relate to ourselves with kindness and acceptance as opposed to getting stuck in fear and self-loathing.
- Helps foster inner calm and balance, composure, ground-edness and relaxation.
- We learn to surf our thoughts, feelings, emotions rather than being swamped by them.
- Refines consciousness so that we can see more subtle aspects of our experience. This leads to insight and clarity about the nature of our experience.
- Energizes body and mind.

Body Scan

A body scan brings you into the present moment using the physical body as an 'anchor'. There are many body scans available online. Alternatively you can record the following scan onto your tablet/ipod/phone and play it back to yourself.

Lie down on your back somewhere comfortable. Have your arms slightly away from the sides of the body with the palms facing upwards. You might need a small pillow under your head. Take the chin to the chest to lengthen the back of the neck and then release it. Soften your face. Make sure you are comfortable.

There is nothing else to do, nowhere else to go. Everything can wait. You are using this time for a body scan.

Slowly close the eyes and place your awareness on your breathing. Feel your body being breathed.

Now take three deeper breaths than normal. Inhale deeply through the nose and exhale completely. Again inhale and exhale. Once more a nice deep inhale and a long, complete exhale.

Now go back to normal breathing, breathing softly in and out through the nose. Just breathing.

Now bring your attention to your feet. Be aware of any sensations in the toes. Just be aware of any sensations and let them be.

Be aware of the soles of the feet. Just be aware of any sensations and let them be.

Be aware of the tops of the feet. Just let them be as they are.

Now become aware of your ankles, your calves and then your shins. Notice any sensations there.

What is happening in the front of your knees? And the back of your knees.

Be aware of any sensations in your thighs... the back of your legs and up into the hips. Just be aware of any sensations but don't attach to them.

Feel your bottom being supported by the bed or the floor. Does one side feel heavier or more supported than the other side or do both sides of the body feel equal? Just notice. There's no need to move, shift or adjust your body.

Bring your attention to your back, noticing which parts of your back are in contact with the floor or bed. Again notice whether one side feels heavier or more supported than the other side.

What about your spine? Where does that make contact with the floor or bed?

How does your tummy feel? Is it soft and relaxed or is it tense? Be aware of the rise and fall of your tummy as the breath enters and leaves your body. Don't attach to it. Just notice it.

Move your awareness up to your chest, feeling the chest open as the breath passes through. Feel the breath breathing you.

Notice the arms and how heavy they feel. Do both arms feel equally heavy?

If you find your mind is wandering that's okay. Just gently bring your attention back to the body and to the hands. Are there any sensations in the palms, any tingling or heat?

Bring your awareness to the fingers. Can you feel your finger nails?

Now focus on your shoulders, being aware of how they feel.

Breathe... keep breathing and allow your attention to scan the neck and the throat. Draw your awareness towards your face, to the chin and the jaw.

Observe whether there is any tension in your tongue and feel what is happening in your nose. Put your attention on the breath entering and leaving your nostrils. Maybe one nostril feels more open than the other? Just observe it and accept whatever is happening.

What do the eyeballs behind the closed eyes feel like?

Notice which part of the back of your head is in contact with the floor.

Breathe. Feel your body resting gently on the floor. Just breathe. Be aware of any sensations and just accept them. Feel your body being breathed. Stay where you are for as long as you like.

When you feel like finishing this practice, take three deeper breaths than normal, roll over onto your side and come to a sitting position.

Top Tips from Meditators

I used to think that I was useless at meditating. I would sit there and my thoughts would be all over the place and each time I caught myself thinking I would say to myself, 'See, you can't meditate, your mind keeps thinking about things so what's the point?'

Now, when I catch myself thinking I say, 'Hey, well done, you have become aware of the fact that you are lost in thought so now you can bring your attention back to the breath.'

Just that small shift in attitude has helped me so much. (Hilary)

I thought I couldn't meditate because I have a bad leg and hip so I can't sit upright. Then my teacher told me I could lie down to meditate as long as my spine was straight. She said that the drawback of meditating lying down is that I might fall asleep so she suggested that I lie with my knees bent up, slightly apart, feet on the floor. In this way, if I start to drop off my legs fall to one side and wake me up. (James)

Just meditate. Even if you don't feel like it, just do it. At first I hardly ever felt like doing it. I would much rather have been doing something else. But once I acknowledged that feeling of resistance and told myself to 'just do it' it felt like I had overcome a hurdle. That feeling of resistance passed after a few weeks and now I find I want (and need!) to meditate. (Jo)

I have a meditation app on my phone that 'dings' every couple of minutes to remind me to bring my focus back to the breath. It's really helpful because my mind always wanders during meditation. The app is called Zazen. (Lou)

I'm a restless person so I find it difficult to sit still. For me, walking meditation works best. I just walk slowly and deliberately and mindfully. It stills my mind in the same way that sitting meditation does. (Liam)

This might sound a bit childish but it worked for me! I have a calendar on the side of the fridge and each time I sit down and meditate for 15 minutes I tick the chart. In this way I have a visual record that helps me to keep focused on my practice. (Debbie)

Mindfulness and meditation can be practiced anywhere. I stand and focus on my breathing at the bus stop every morning. Instead of getting stressed about the bus being late, I welcome the opportunity to have this extra time to focus on my practice. (Ed)

I was suffering from depression and my doctor sent me for MBCT. Now I'm a regular meditator. I can't do without it. I recommend MBCT as a way to get into mindful meditation. (Peter)

Some days I would sit to meditate on my breath for 20 minutes and at the end of the session I would realize that after the initial minute or two of watching my breathing I had done nothing but get lost in thought. I used to think I had wasted my time by sitting meditating but then I began to say to myself, 'You had the intention of meditating. Well done for trying. Try again tomorrow.' The more I practiced, the easier it got. So my tip is to keep going because it's worth it in the end. (Tara)

My main difficulty was having the self-discipline to take a meager 20 minutes out of my day to meditate. Then I joined a 'virtual' meditation group online. We meet in a meditation space on a site called 'Second Life' to meditate together. This has really helped me because I enjoy the feeling of being part of a group. I feel that I'm letting the group down if I miss the scheduled meeting time so that motivates me to keep up with my practice. (Clare)

Each time I closed my eyes to meditate I just wanted to fall asleep. Then someone told me about this app with a white dot that you watch as it gets bigger and smaller. I don't know why, but that worked for me. Maybe it's because I have to keep my eyes open. It's called the dotout app. (Iain)

I started with 5 minutes a day instead of 20 minutes. Then on Saturday and Sunday I did 20 minutes but 5 a day during the week. When I added that up I was doing over an hour of meditation a week. So I would say just do 5 minutes to start with. (John)

I sit for the first 10 minutes and let all my thoughts come up and I even write down some of them. That helps to get them out of the way. Then I spend the next 10 minutes focusing on my breath. (Ricky)

I'm a busy mum of three so finding time to meditate isn't easy. The kids come out of school at 3:30pm so now I leave home at 3pm and park the car in a quiet space near the school and use that time for meditation. I just sit in the car. Sometimes I use a guided meditation on my ipod, other times I just focus on the breath. This works perfectly for me because it has now become part of my daily routine. (Alex)

When my thoughts arise I imagine them as clouds in a blue sky. I allow them to drift by and I don't hold on to them. This image has really helped me in my meditation practice. (Ty)

Glossary

11:11: Spiritual wake-up call.

12 steps: See Twelve Steps.

AA: See Twelve Steps.

ABET: Asian Biological Energy Therapy. This is a combination of several oriental holistic healing techniques that are all non-invasive. Bio-Energetics is believed to restore the patient's natural energy fields and can have a positive effect on the emotional, physical and spiritual well-being.

ADD: See ADHD.

ADHD: Attention deficit hyperactivity disorder. ADHD is a group of behavioral symptoms that include inattentiveness, hyperactivity and impulsiveness. Attention deficit disorder (ADD) is a sub-type of ADHD. Common symptoms of ADHD include a short attention span, restlessness or constant fidgeting and being easily distracted.

AEROSOL: Aerosols are used as an inhalant by breathing the chemicals in through one's nose or mouth. Effects include dizziness, intoxicated behavior, stomach pain, headaches and hallucinations.

AGORAPHOBIA: A pathological fear of being in public places. This sometimes results in the sufferer becoming housebound.

ALCOHOLICS ANONYMOUS: See Twelve Steps.

AMPHETAMINES: The name amphetamine refers to a whole group of manmade stimulant drugs. They speed up your mind and body so they are commonly known as speed. Street speed usually comes as a white or off-white powder.

ANTABUSE/ANTIBUSE: Is an alcohol-abuse deterrent. It works by blocking the breakdown of alcohol, causing unpleasant side effects such as vomiting or upset stomach when any alcohol is consumed.

ASIAN BIO-ENERGETIC THERAPY: See ABET.

AYAHUASCA: Ayahuasca is a psychedelic brew of various plant infusions prepared with the banisteriopsis vine. Many people who have taken ayahuasca report having gained deep insights into the nature of reality. Some report that they gain access to higher spiritual dimensions and make contact with various spiritual or extra-dimensional beings who can act as guides or healers.

AZ: Arizona.

BENZOS: See hypnotics.

BIPOLAR: Bipolar disorder used to be called manic depression. Someone with bipolar disorder will have severe mood swings. These can last several weeks or months.

BODY SCAN: A body scan is a component of mindfulness meditation. The aim is to allow yourself to experience how each part of the body feels, without trying to change anything. Just being with what is there.

BORDERLINE: Borderline personality disorder is characterized by a tendency to act impulsively and without consideration of the consequences. The mood is unpredictable and there is emotional instability, a tendency to outbursts of emotion and an incapacity to control the behavioral explosions. There can be quarrelsome behavior and conflicts with others, especially when impulsive acts are thwarted. The borderline type has a tendency to self-destructive behavior, including suicide gestures and attempts.

BREAKBEAT: Electronic music with a distinct percussive rhythm.

CBT: Cognitive Behavioral Therapy is a talking therapy that can help you manage your problems by changing the way you think and behave. It has been shown to be particularly helpful at tackling problems such as anxiety, depression, post-traumatic stress disorder (PTSD) and drug misuse. Unlike other types of talking treatments such as psychotherapy, CBT deals with your current problems rather than focusing on issues from your past. It works by helping you make sense of overwhelming problems by breaking them down into smaller parts.

CHRISTIAN EVANGELIST: An evangelical Christian is a believer in Jesus Christ who is faithful in sharing and promoting the 'good news'.

COCAINE: Also known as coke. It is a white powder that comes from the coca plant. It is usually snorted but can also be injected or swallowed. It is highly addictive. It speeds up the way your mind and body works. The buzz lasts for up to an hour but is followed by an immediate comedown.

CODEPENDENCY: Codependency refers to the dependence on the needs of, or control of, another person. Codependency can occur in any type of relationship, including family, work, friendship and also romantic relationships.

COLD TURKEY: The sudden and abrupt giving up of a habit or addiction rather than gradually easing the process through gradual reduction or by using replacement medication.

CRACK: Crack cocaine is the form of cocaine that can be smoked. It is said to be the most addictive form of cocaine.

CRACK HOUSE: A crack house is a building where drug dealers and drug users buy, sell, produce and use illegal drugs, including, but not limited to, crack cocaine.

CRANIO-SACRAL: Cranio-sacral therapy (CST) is a form of bodywork or alternative therapy that regulates the flow of cerebrospinal fluid by using therapeutic touch to manipulate the synarthrodial joints of the cranium. To do this, a practitioner will apply light touches to a patient's skull, face, spine and pelvis.

CRYSTAL METH: Crystal meth is like a very powerful form of speed, and it is usually smoked. It produces a rush at first which is initially like crack but the effects of it last much longer than crack does – from 2 to 12 hours. After use there is a marked comedown effect where you feel flat and washed out. The more you use, the worse the comedowns. Crystal meth is very addictive.

CUPPING: Cupping therapy is an ancient Chinese form of

medicine. Glass cups are heated and placed on the skin (usually on the back). Suction is created on the skin and this is thought to improve blood flow in order to promote healing.

DHAPERAZINE: Dhaperazine is a drug used for the short-term management of anxiety. It is also used to manage mood and behavioral changes in some psychiatric conditions such as schizophrenia and psychosis.

DIANETICS: Dianetics was created by L. Ron Hubbard and is practiced by followers of Scientology. Dianetics divides the mind into three parts: the conscious analytical mind, the subconscious reactive mind and thirdly the somatic mind. The goal of Dianetics is to remove the reactive (subconscious) mind by a procedure called auditing. Auditing is a process whereby a series of questions are asked by the Scientology auditor, in an attempt to rid the audited person of the painful experiences of the past.

DIAZEPAM: Diazepam belongs to a class of medicines called benzodiazepines. It helps to control feelings of anxiety and make people feel less agitated. Diazepam can cause tolerance, dependence and even withdrawal symptoms in some people. The effects of diazepam may last for a few hours or even days after you stop taking it.

DIAZEPINES: See hypnotics.

DTs: Delirium Tremens is Latin for 'shaking frenzy'. It's acute physical shaking caused by withdrawing from alcohol.

ECSTASY: Also known as 'E'. It is the most common club drug. It usually comes as a tablet but occasionally it comes as a white powder. It can make you feel full of energy and love but it has different effects on different people. It can also make you anxious, frightened and paranoid. The after-effects of E can leave you feeling flat, washed out and tired. This feeling can last for several days.

EFFEXOR: Venlafaxine (brand name: Effexor or Efexor) is an antidepressant for the treatment of major depressive disorder and as a treatment for anxiety or depression. It is a very commonly prescribed antidepressant but could have a link to an increased suicide risk.

EMDR: Eye Movement Desensitization and Reprocessing is a psychotherapy developed by Francine Shapiro. It alleviates the symptoms of unresolved trauma using side-to-side eye movements rather like REM. Rapid eye movement (REM) sleep is a stage of sleep characterized by the rapid and random movement of the eyes. REM sleep is associated with dreaming.

ENNEAGRAM: The Enneagram defines nine basic personality types of human nature. It offers a framework for understanding yourself and others. Therapists, business counselors, human resource directors and spiritual seekers from around the world are all finding the Enneagram to be immensely useful for self-understanding and personal growth. Rather than 'putting you in a box' the Enneagram shows you the box you are in and the way out. www.enneagraminstitute.com www.Ennea.com

FELDENKRAIS: The Feldenkrais Method® is an approach to learning and action through the medium of movement. Subtle exercises and movements improve movement, posture and breathing. It is named after its originator, Moshe Feldenkrais (1904–1984).

FREEZE MECHANISM: When the fight or flight systems cannot be activated, escape is impossible physically or relationally, fighting is not an option for all sorts of reasons, or the traumatic threat is prolonged, the limbic system of the brain can simultaneously activate the parasympathetic branch of the autonomic nervous system, causing a state of freezing called 'tonic immobility' – like a mouse going dead when caught by a cat, or like a deer caught in headlights.

HALFWAY HOUSE: A halfway house is a place where convicted criminals, alcoholics and drug addicts can stay while they begin the process of reintegration into society.

HASH: Hash is the resin collected from the flowers of the cannabis plant. Hash is usually smoked in pipes, water pipes, joints and hookahs, sometimes mixed with cannabis flowers or tobacco. It can also be eaten. The most common effects of hash and cannabis are a sense of well-being and relaxation, an increased appreciation of music, heightened senses, sleepiness, pain relief, nausea relief and increased appetite. There are also several negative effects including dry mouth, rapid heartbeat, impaired short-term memory, anxiety and panic attacks. Sometimes called dope/weed/pot/skunk.

HEROIN: Heroin is a drug made from morphine, which is extracted from the opium poppy.

HIV: HIV stands for Human Immunodeficiency Virus.

HOPONOPO: Hoponopo is a Hawaiian healing process that involves repeating the statements: I Love You, I'm Sorry, Please Forgive Me, Thank You. It is based on the idea that loving yourself is the greatest way to improve yourself, and as you improve yourself, you improve your world.

HUNGRY GHOST RETREATS: These mindful recovery retreats are offered as an opportunity to experience a wholly Buddhist approach to recovery from all forms of addiction. Retreats are open to those new to recovery as a support to their ongoing abstinence. http://www.hungryghostretreats.org/

HYPNOTICS: Hypnotics are prescribed for insomnia. These drugs include benzodiazepines and non-benzodiazepines. Hypnotics should only be taken under a doctor's direction. They may be unsafe when mixed with alcohol or with each other. Taking hypnotics with alcohol or with each other can lead to excessive drowsiness and even death.

INNER CRITIC: The inner critic is a concept used in popular psychology to refer to a sub-personality that judges and demeans a person. The inner critic is usually experienced as an inner voice attacking a person, saying that he or she is bad, wrong, inadequate, worthless, guilty, and so on.

INTUITIVE THERAPIST: A counselor who works with his/her intuition, sometimes along with psychic abilities.

KETAMINE: Is often referred to as 'the horse tranquilizer'. It is chemically related to phencyclidine (PCP) and it is widely used as a veterinary and a human anesthetic. At lower doses the effects include a sense of euphoria and may involve mild hallucinations. At higher doses vivid hallucinations are common.

LITHIUM: Lithium is used to treat the manic episodes of manic depression. Manic symptoms include hyperactivity, rushed speech, poor judgment, reduced need for sleep, aggression and anger. It also helps to prevent or lessen the intensity of manic episodes.

LSD: Lysergic Acid Diethylamide. LSD is a potent, mood-changing chemical. It is manufactured from lysergic acid, which is found in a fungus. It is odorless, colorless and has a slightly bitter taste. Commonly known as acid, it is sold in small tablets, capsules or gelatin squares (window panes). An LSD experience is called a trip and can last as long as 12 hours.

LUTHERAN: Lutheranism is a major branch of Western Christianity that identifies with the theology of Martin Luther, a German monk and theologian.

MAGIC MUSHROOMS: See psychedelic mushrooms.

MBCT: Mindfulness Based Cognitive Therapy. See CBT.

MBSR: See mindfulness.

METH: Short for crystal meth.

METHADONE: If you are addicted to heroin it means that you develop withdrawal symptoms within a day or so of the last dose. These can be quite severe. Methadone is a drug that is similar to heroin, although it lasts a lot longer in the body. It is usually prescribed by a doctor to those patients who are giving up heroin because taking methadone lessens the withdrawal symptoms.

MINDFULNESS: Mindfulness is being aware of thoughts, feelings, bodily sensations and surrounding environment in every moment and accepting whatever is there without judging whether they are right or wrong. Although it has roots in

Buddhist meditation the practice of mindfulness has entered the mainstream through MBSR (Mindfulness-Based Stress Reduction). Programs based on MBSR have been widely adapted in schools, prisons, hospitals and other environments.

NA: See Narcotics Anonymous.

NARCOTICS ANONYMOUS: NA is a non-profit fellowship for recovering addicts who meet regularly to support each other in recovery. There is only ONE requirement for membership: the desire to stop using the addictive substance. There are no fees, no pledges to sign, no promises to make to anyone. They are not connected to any political, religious or law enforcement groups. Anyone may join, regardless of age, race, sexual identity, creed, religion or lack of religion.

NLF: New Life Foundation.

NOBLE SILENCE: Listening takes place not just through the ears, but with all the senses. Noble Silence traditionally begins with a vow to keep silent for a specific period of time. It can be an hour, a day, a week or a month. There are practitioners who have kept Noble Silence for years.

NVC (NONVIOLENT COMMUNICATION): Nonviolent Communication is a process of communication, developed by psychologist Marshall Rosenberg, that is based on compassion, authenticity and courage. Also sometimes known as Compassionate Communication.

OCD: Obsessive compulsive disorder is a mental health condition where a person has obsessive thoughts and compulsive behavior. A compulsion is a repetitive behavior or mental act that someone feels they need to carry out to try to prevent an obsession coming true.

OPIATES: Opiates are a group of drugs that are derived from opium which comes from the poppy plant. Opiates produce a sense of well-being or euphoria that can become addictive. Even when used legitimately for pain relief, many people develop tolerance and can go on to develop an addiction to opiates.

PANHANDLING: Slang term for begging.

PARANOIA: Everybody experiences suspicious or irrational thoughts from time to time. These fears are described as paranoid when they are exaggerated and there is no evidence that they are true. Generally speaking, if you are experiencing paranoia, you will feel a sense of threat and fear.

PCP: See phencyclidine.

PHENCYCLIDINE: Phencyclidine is a synthetic dissociative drug. It was developed in the 1950s as a surgical anesthetic. Use of PCP in humans was discontinued in 1965 because it was found that patients often became agitated, delusional and irrational while recovering from its anesthetic effects. At high doses, PCP can cause nausea, vomiting, blurred vision, flicking up and down of the eyes, drooling, loss of balance, dizziness, hallucinations, seizures, coma and even death.

POST-TRAUMATIC STRESS: See PTS/PTSD.

POT: See hash.

PROZAC: Prozac is a type of antidepressant.

PSYCHEDELIC MUSHROOMS: Also known as 'Magic Mushrooms', these are mushrooms that contain the psychedelic drugs psilocybin and psilocin. Many cultures have used these mushrooms in religious rites. These days they are used recreationally for their psychedelic effects.

PSYCHOLOGICAL FUSION: A state where the differentiation between self and others will recede or disappear.

PTS/PTSD: Post-traumatic stress disorder is an anxiety disorder that can develop following one or more traumatic events. The diagnosis of PTSD may be given when a group of symptoms such as disturbing recurring flashbacks, avoidance or numbing of memories of the event, and high levels of anxiety continue for more than a month after the traumatic event.

REIKI: Reiki is a Japanese technique for stress reduction, relaxation and healing. It is based on the idea that an unseen life-force energy flows through us. If one's life-force energy is low, then we are more likely to get sick or feel stress, and if it is high we are more capable of being happy and healthy.

RITALIN: Ritalin (methylphenidate) is a central nervous system stimulant. It affects chemicals in the brain and nerves that contribute to hyperactivity and impulse control. It is used to treat attention deficit disorder (ADD) and attention deficit hyperactivity disorder (ADHD).

SADAS: Sadas is an independent charity which offers advice and information about alcohol. The charity (based in the south of England) works within the recovery agenda. www.sadas.org.uk

SCIENTOLOGY: See Dianetics.

SEROXAT: Seroxat is used to treat a variety of mental health problems including depression, panic disorder, anxiety disorder, obsessive compulsive disorder and post-traumatic stress disorder. In some people it can intensify depression and suicidal feelings in the early stages of treatment, thereby increasing the risk of self-harm or suicide. As Seroxat starts to work these risks decrease.

SKUNK: See hash.

SMART RECOVERY: Helps individuals seeking abstinence from addictive behaviors to gain independence, achieve recovery and lead meaningful and satisfying lives. They teach self-empowerment and self-reliance. They provide meetings that are educational, supportive and focused on open discussions. They support the use of prescribed medications and psychological treatments where appropriate. The Smart Recovery approach can be used to tackle any form of addictive behavior, including drugs, alcohol and gambling. www.smartrecovery.org.uk/

SOLVENTS: See aerosol.

SPEED: See amphetamines.

STEAM BATH DETOX: Steam baths are a fast and effective way to detox. The body gets rid of wastes and toxins through urine, sweat, faeces and exhaled air. A steam session capitalizes on the body's ability to sweat toxins away. It is an effortless and practical way to detox.

SUBUTEX: Is an opioid drug that is similar to heroin. It can be prescribed to help to reduce cravings for heroin. The drug most commonly prescribed as a substitute for heroin is methadone. However, Subutex (buprenorphine) is still a good treatment and some people prefer it because it tends to be easier to come off than methadone. Some people take methadone long term for maintenance and then switch to Subutex if they decide to detox. Subutex tablets are placed beneath the tongue, where they are absorbed directly into the bloodstream.

SUSTAINABILITY: Sustainability is based on a simple principle: Everything that we need for our survival and well-being depends on our natural environment. Sustainability creates and maintains the conditions under which humans and nature can exist in productive harmony, that permit fulfilling the social, economic and other requirements of present and future generations.

TEGRETOL: Tegretol is a prescription medicine used to treat certain types of seizures and certain types of nerve pain.

THAMKRABOK: Thamkrabok Monastery in Thailand offers a highly successful herbal detoxification service to drug-addicted persons from around the world. Although based on the Buddhist faith and principles, people from all denominations and ethnic groups are welcomed. See Resources.

THORAZINE: Thorazine (chlorpromazine) is a mood stabilizer drug used for treating bipolar disorder. It is especially useful in those with long years or decades of illness because they are now more prone to depressive episodes than manic episodes.

TONGLEN: Tonglen is Tibetan for 'giving and taking' (or sending and receiving), and refers to a meditation practice found in Tibetan Buddhism.

TRACK MARKS: The darkening of the veins due to scarring and toxin build-up produces tracks along the length of the veins that are known as track marks.

TRAUMA CLINIC: A Trauma Clinic is a treatment facility for those who are experiencing psychological or emotional problems as a result of serious adverse events.

TRE: Tension and Trauma Releasing Exercises. TRE is a set of six exercises that help to release deep tension from the body by evoking a self-controlled muscular shaking process in the body called neurogenic muscle tremors. The exercises are a simple form of stretching and are used to gently trigger these voluntary muscle tremors. It is an effective method for releasing the symptoms of stress, tension and anxiety from overwhelming events.

TREMOR RELEASE: See TRE.

TWELVE STEPS: This program is a set of guiding principles outlining a course of action for recovery from addiction, compulsion or other behavioral problems. As summarized by Alcoholics Anonymous (also known as AA), the process involves the following:

- admitting that one cannot control one's addiction or compulsion;
- recognizing a Higher Power that can give strength;
- examining past errors with the help of a sponsor (experienced member);
- making amends for these errors;
- learning to live a new life with a new code of behavior;
- helping others who suffer from the same addictions or compulsions.

UPPERS: Uppers are stimulant drugs that induce enhanced alertness and wakefulness. They give users an 'up' feeling which is why they are referred to as 'uppers'. Stimulants are widely used throughout the world both with and without prescription.

VALIUM: A narcotic sedative commonly used to treat muscle spasm and anxiety. Valium is also known as diazepam.

VINCE CULLEN: See Hungry Ghost Retreats.

WORKAHOLICS ANONYMOUS: Workaholics Anonymous is a

fellowship of individuals who share their experience, strength and hope with each other so that they may solve their common problems and help others to recover from workaholism. The only requirement for membership is the desire to stop working compulsively.

WORKAWAY: Workaway is a volunteer website introducing working travelers and language learners with like-minded hosts. www.workaway.info

WWOOF: WWOOF organizations link people who want to volunteer on organic farms or smallholdings with people who are looking for volunteer help. In return for volunteer help, WWOOF hosts offer food, accommodation and opportunities to learn about organic lifestyles. www.wwoof.net

XANAX: Xanax (alprazolam) belongs to a group of drugs called benzodiazepines. It works by slowing down the movement of chemicals in the brain that may become unbalanced. This results in a reduction in nervous tension (anxiety). It is used to treat anxiety disorders, panic disorders, and anxiety caused by depression.

YABA: Yaba is a stimulant that includes caffeine, vanilla flavorings and bulking agents along with meth. It's usually smoked off tinfoil and the user inhales vanilla-scented vapor. Burma (also known as Myanmar) is the largest producer of yaba. It is a highly addictive substance.

Resources

Thamkrabok Monastery:
http://wat-thamkrabok.org/
The Thamkrabok Monastery in Thailand has for over 50 years provided a highly successful herbal detoxification service to drug-addicted persons from around the world. Although based on the Buddhist faith and principles, people from all denominations and ethnic groups are welcomed.

Dharma Seed: Downloadable meditation teachings
http://www.dharmaseed.org/
Dharma Seed has collected and distributed dharma talks by teachers transmitting the Vipassana or Insight practices of Theravada Buddhism, the oldest Buddhist tradition still actively pursued in the 21st century.

Stephen and Martine Batchelor:
http://stephenbatchelor.org
Stephen and Martine Batchelor are Buddhist teachers and authors who live in south-west France and conduct meditation retreats and seminars worldwide. The website includes a multitude of materials that offer a broad introduction to their work.

Tricycle:
http://www.tricycle.com/
Tricycle is a website, magazine, blog, wisdom collection, gallery and a community to create a platform for exploring contemporary and historic Buddhist activity around the world.

5th Precept: Mindfulness and recovery
http://www.5th-precept.org/
The 5th Precept group supports the use of Buddhist teachings,
traditions and practices to help people recover from the suffering
caused by addictive behaviors.

UCSD Center for Mindfulness:
http://health.ucsd.edu/specialties/mindfulness/Pages/default.as
px
The Center for Mindfulness at the University of California in San
Diego is a multifaceted program of clinical care, professional
training, education and research intended to further the practice
and integration of mindfulness into the lives of individuals.

Mindful Psychology:
http://www.mindfulpsychology.com/
This is the website of Dr. Thomas Bien, a licensed psychologist,
author and mindfulness teacher. His psychology background
includes extensive clinical practice and research in the field of
addictive behavior.

Mind and Life Institute:
http://www.mindandlife.org
The Mind and Life Institute has pioneered the field of contemplative science and operates in an array of rigorous fields –
neuroscience, psychology, education, medicine, ethics, religion,
the humanities.

The Greater Good Science Center:
http://greatergood.berkeley.edu
Based at University of California Berkeley, The Greater Good
Science Center studies the psychology, sociology and neuroscience of well-being, and teaches skills that foster a thriving,
resilient and compassionate society.

The Positive Psychology Center:
http://www.ppc.sas.upenn.edu
The Positive Psychology Center (PPC) at the University of
Pennsylvania promotes research, training, education and the
dissemination of Positive Psychology. The PPC is internationally
recognized for empirical studies in Positive Psychology and
resilience.

Plum Village Mindfulness Practice Center:
http://plumvillage.org
Plum Village is a Buddhist meditation center in the Dordogne, in
southern France. It was founded by Vietnamese Zen master Thich
Nhat Hanh, and his colleague Bhikkhuni Chan Khong, in 1982.

Further Reading

Thomas Bien, *Mindful Therapy*
Mindful Therapy is a welcome addition to the literature for psychotherapists, occupational therapists, therapists-in-training and other types of teachers. A highly readable balance of theoretical groundwork, personal experience, case studies and practice exercises, the book offers ways to bring the teachings of Buddhism into a psychotherapeutic practice, and provides a thorough explanation of the benefits of doing so.

Martine Batchelor, *Meditation for Life*
Using words and photographs, this book shows how meditation can enrich your life. This book looks at the three main Buddhist traditions – Tibetan, Theravadan and Zen – and offers step-by-step guides to meditation on a variety of themes. Each chapter discusses one of the many different approaches to meditation and features practical instructions and exercises, as well as a discussion of a related aspect of Buddhism, such as wisdom or non-attachment.

Jack Kornfield, *The Wise Heart*
Offers practical tools for coping with modern life and dealing with emotions such as fear, anger and shame. Kornfield also shares the illuminating stories of his students and fellow practitioners, as well as his own journey towards enlightenment, including his recovery from a violence-filled childhood.

Rick Hanson, *Buddha's Brain*
Jesus, Moses, Muhammad, Gandhi and the Buddha all had brains built essentially like anyone else's, yet they were able to harness their thoughts and shape their patterns of thinking in ways that changed history. With new breakthroughs in modern neuro-

science and the wisdom of thousands of years of contemplative practice, it is possible for us to shape our own thoughts in a similar way for greater happiness, love, compassion and wisdom.

Pema Chödrön, *When Things Fall Apart*
This accessible guide to compassionate living shows us how we can use painful emotions to cultivate wisdom, compassion and courage, ways of communication that lead to openness and true intimacy with others, practices for reversing our negative habitual patterns, methods for working with chaotic situations, and ways to cultivate compassionate, energetic social action.

Thomas Bien, *The Buddha's Way of Happiness*
Through mindfulness we learn to live with our emotions, thoughts, cravings and urges without getting caught up in them, without being enslaved by them. Mindfulness helps us understand what lies at the root of our behavior and thus it has the power to transform negative habits.

Thomas and Beverly Bien, *Finding the Center Within*
All of us want to live a calmer, more peaceful existence. Thomas and Beverly Bien teach that if we find the center within through ongoing mindfulness, we will have the capacity to live deeply and fully – with boundless peace and happiness – in any external circumstance. We can learn to be calm in the midst of the storm.

Steven F. Hick and Thomas Bien, *Mindfulness and the Therapeutic Relationship*
Grounded in research, chapters demonstrate how therapists' own mindfulness practice can help them to listen more attentively and be more fully present. Leading proponents of different treatment approaches illustrate a variety of ways that mindfulness principles can complement standard techniques and improve outcomes by strengthening the connection between therapist and client.

Thomas Bien, *Mindful Recovery: A Spiritual Path to Healing from Addiction*
Drawing on both ancient spiritual wisdom and the authors' extensive clinical psychological work with their patients over many years, *Mindful Recovery* shows you how to use the simple Buddhist practice of mindfulness to be aware of – and enjoy – life in the present moment without the need to enhance or avoid experience with addictive behaviors.

Thich Nhat Hanh, *Peace Is Every Step*
Contains commentaries and meditations, personal anecdotes and stories from Nhat Hanh's experiences as a peace activist, teacher, and community leader. It begins where the reader already is – in the kitchen, office, driving a car, walking in a park – and shows how deep meditative presence is available now.

Martin Seligman, *Authentic Happiness*
Argues that happiness can be a learned and cultivated behavior, explaining how every person possesses at least five of 24 profiled strengths that can be built on in order to improve life.

AYNI
BOOKS

"Ayni" is a Quechua word meaning "reciprocity" – sharing, giving and receiving – whatever you give out comes back to you. To be in Ayni is to be in balance, harmony and right relationship with oneself and nature, of which we are all an intrinsic part. Complementary and Alternative approaches to health and well-being essentially follow a holistic model, within which one is given support and encouragement to move towards a state of balance, true health and wholeness, ultimately leading to the awareness of one's unique place in the Universal jigsaw of life – Ayni, in fact.